LIVING THE BRAND

how to transform every member of your organization into a brand champion

NICHOLAS IND

IN ASSOCIATION WITH

Marketing

KOGAN PAGE

First published in 2001

Kogan Page
120 Pentonville Road
London N1 9JN
UK

Kogan Page
163 Central Avenue, Suite 2
Dover NH 03820
USA

British Library Cataloguing in Publication Data

A CIP record for this book is available from the British Library.

ISBN 0 7494 3351 5

Typeset by Saxon Graphics Ltd, Derby
Printed and bound by Creative Print and Design (Wales), Ebbw Vale

contents

acknowledgements

I would like to thank the following people for their help with this book: Andreas Gronqvist for designing the charts and graphs (at least the better looking ones – the others are mine), Joanna Rembielinska Nolke for the e-learning illustrations, Phil Rushton of Icon Medialab, Matthew Bell of VSO, Milorad Ajder of DRC International, Elodie Boyer of Carré Noir, Dr Onno Maathuis of Positioneringsgroep, Dr Klaus Schmidt of Henrion Ludlow and Schmidt and Maria Chiara Riondino of Accenture.

I would also like to thank those people who gave up their time to be interviewed: Chip Bell, Lu Setnicka, Hal Arneson and Chris Van Dyke of Patagonia, Nelson Farris of Nike, Larry Keeley of Doblin Group, Dr Karen Beuk of Rabobank, Dr Paul Kwakkenbos of PinkRoccade, Shelly Wheeler of Shell, Marcus Atkins of Trailfinders, Christopher Lochhead of Scient, Robert Lilja of Infercor, Melissa Dyrdahl of Adobe, Peter Vroom of QM Communicatie, Frank Nigriello of Unipart and Geerd Schlangen of Origin.

Nicholas Ind
January 2001

Introduction

Living the Brand is about how organizations empower and enthuse their employees. The core argument is that this is best achieved by articulating a sense of the organization that is credible and motivating both internally and externally. However, simply stating the organization's purpose and values by themselves is not enough. Organizations need to build meaning into the ideas so that employees can genuinely live the brand in their day-to-day lives. This is increasingly important if businesses and government and voluntary organizations want to make best use of the intellectual resources of all of their employees; to capture the most innovative ideas; to build strong and lasting relationships with customers; to use the enthusiasm and imagination of people.

The book is aimed at communication and marketing professionals and human resources personnel who are interested in the potential benefits of engaging the employees of an organization in the imaginative pursuit of a common cause. It demonstrates why this is important to individuals and organizations and how this can best be delivered. The idea of engaging employees may seem a simple one but it is hard to achieve in practice because it cannot be ordered and controlled. Rather it requires practitioners to work within the cultural framework of the organization; it involves the creation of a rational and emotional idea that enthuses employees and helps deliver organizational goals.

One of the keys to a book of this sort is to find good and interesting examples. Overall, I have tried to avoid the frequently cited organizations that appear in most business texts. Instead I have sought out organizations that others and I believe have some real insight into the problems of articulating and then delivering brands through people. To provide a flavour of the power of a company that seems to do this well, the book starts with a story about a very distinctive organization – Patagonia – which believes that business should be used to further environmental causes. However, this alternative stance is not the rationale for its inclusion. Rather the example shows how values emerge out of a founder's beliefs and an organization's memory. When values are deep rooted – as they seem to be at Patagonia – they have the power of authenticity. They guide decision making from the fundamental (the policy on quality) to the incidental (organic food in the canteen) not because there is some command and control structure that dictates it but because people believe in the ideas behind the values.

Having used a specific example to illustrate the general concept, the book will look at the nature of branding and why people have become such important definers of the brand. Underlying this discussion is the sense that both individuals and organizations need values. It is essential to their wellbeing and their sense of worth.

The final part of the book looks at the best methods for articulating brand ideas and for embedding them into the organization. This section, in particular, will cite examples of best practice from around the world and provide readers with ideas and templates that they can adapt for their own organizations.

I'm
genuinely
feeling
groovy

Meet Chip Bell: 11 times world freestyle Frisbee champion, occasional surfing instructor and receptionist for outdoor clothing company, Patagonia. Based in Ventura, California, Patagonia is an organization with a very distinctive culture. Not only does it employ a world Frisbee champion to answer the phone and greet people – it also has a clear philosophy, born out of the organization's earliest days. This is an $180 million turnover company, where the founder and chief executive conducts job interviews while surfing and employees are trained to abseil from building tops unfurling environmental protest banners. A company where workers leave their desks for the beach when the waves are over six feet and where the stores have been picketed by the Christian Action Council. It is a powerful brand that has a demonstrable commitment to quality, an idiosyncratic point of view, devoted customers and devoutly passionate employees. It has an influence, particularly in the United States, far larger than its size would suggest and serves as a model for how business can have a genuine and positive impact on the environment. Patagonia is a standard bearer for an 'employe ecentric approach' that stresses the value of engaging people with the organization they work for and stimulating them to live the brand.

The story of Patagonia

Yvon Chouinard, a French Canadian who grew up in Burbank, California, founded the company that became Patagonia in 1958. As a young man he was a keen surfer and climber. He also taught himself to be a blacksmith. Using his forging skills, at the age of 18 he started out in business making climbing pitons for himself and then selling a few to friends. This was a job that required absolute precision. Produce a flawed piton and you endanger someone's life. It was not surprising that the young Chouinard had an early obsession with safety and quality. That obsession remained as the company's range of products grew. However, for Chouinard, the business retained a hobbyist culture, albeit a passionate one. The company's first mail order sheet in 1966 noted 'Don't expect speedy delivery in the months of May, June, July, August and September.' This was when Chouinard would close down the forge and go climbing. Winter deliveries could also be interrupted if the surfing was good. Despite this whimsical approach to business, his passionate beliefs helped to galvanize the company and by 1970 it had become the largest supplier of climbing hardware in the United States. This was when Chouinard had his first crisis of conscience. After climbing a peak in Yosemite, called El Capitan, Chouinard recognized the damage that climbers were doing. Pitons have to be hammered in and out of cracks, which disfigures the rockface. On well-trodden routes the environmental damage was clearly noticeable. Chouinard decided that he should set an example to others and he pulled out of the piton business and instead began offering aluminium chocks that could be wedged in by hand. These had long been used by British climbers but were virtually unknown in the United States. Chouinard became an evangelist for 'clean climbing'. The 1972 catalogue contained a 14-page essay on chocks by climber Doug Robinson, who noted that, 'Clean is climbing the rock without changing it; a step closer to organic climbing for the natural man.'

In the mid 1970s, the company moved out of climbing equipment and into outdoor clothing, but the personal philosophy of Chouinard remained a dominant influence. As with climbing gear,

Chouinard's clothing was highly engineered and built to last and there was a distinctive commitment to environmentalism. There was also an ethical stance that encouraged putting principle before profit. This created a corporate culture that was and is against consumption for its own sake. The notion of in-built obsolescence would be anathema to Patagonia. The company actively encourages people to send their clothing in to be repaired when damaged – generally for free – rather than encouraging replacement purchases. Of course, there is a contradiction here in that Patagonia does persuade people to buy its products in the first place and to experience the outdoors – both of which create environmental damage. Chouinard sometimes bemoans the overuse of the wilder areas of the world and the despoliation that occurs but the company cannot have it both ways. All it can do is to try to minimize the damage. For example, when Patagonia was concerned about wasting the scraps left over from the pattern cutting of garments, it created a range of children's clothes from the offcuts. The pieces were oddments so nothing matched, but customers liked the story behind the idea and the range was a success. Most organizations would have capitalized on this, but Patagonia capped its sales and refused to produce additional product to meet demand. Chris Van Dyke, Marketing Director at Patagonia says:

> As a small company we have the leverage to move a large company, because we don't compromise. That creates an incredible power, grossly disproportionate to the revenues we generate. Yvon has always known that being a business model is a huge reason to grow. He's always said that if you do the right thing you'll make money and you also become more powerful.

The environmental cause

Just as Chouinard was an early proselytizer for clean climbing, Patagonia is an advocate for the environment and for persuading other businesses of the importance of environmentalism. This is a company that is not short of opinions and is quite happy about the divisive effect they can have. By having a clear point of view the company creates a closer bond with its customers and employees. There is a sense of active participation in an important cause that matters not just to Patagonia but has the potential to influence the way that people live. This is a campaigning company with a campaigner's zeal. Fostering this seems to be related to the nature of the company's business and the way in which it was founded. Climbing, like many of the outdoor sports with which Patagonia is connected, involves much waiting and then a burst of adrenalin-filled activity. Waiting for salmon to bite, waiting for weather to clear and waiting for the surf is when stories are told. Then, because of the blurring of the boundaries between Patagonia and its customers the stories get retold in Patagonia shops, which tend to be populated by climbers and canoeists and surfers; they get retold in Ventura where employees are passionate sports people; they get retold in advertising; and they get retold in the catalogue in the form of field reports. Here's Gretel Ehrlich, a canoeist, writing from the field:

> I am lying on a sled on the frozen strait just off Cornwallis Island in the Canadian High Arctic. The sun is out; it's always out in May. I'm at the camp of an American seal biologist, Brendan Kelly. We have just been through a three-day storm that almost blew us away. Our water-closet tent vanished first, our food cache is buried deep, our insulated tent is leaning hard though the wind has now calmed. All that is left is ice and light.[1]

This dialogue generated by the relationship with customers is interesting because it is something that happens naturally when companies are small and the managers of a business interact with their customers through their day-to-day work, but it is often hard to sustain as organizations grow. Management becomes removed from the day-to-day realities of a business and as a consequence they lose the direct dialogue and the sense of identification. As Larry Keeley of the Chicago-based, innovation consultancy, Doblin Group says:

> What they're managing (executives) in their heads is an abstraction – something they remember from their one day out

in the field in 1968. Or an abstract understanding of what they think they want a programme to achieve.

People within Patagonia maintain the dialogue naturally because their interests are their customers' – employees are both the producers of goods and active consumers. Stories flow into the company anecdotally or in writing and then flow back out. The stories are not designed to directly sell more products: they're much more to do with building a deep sense of identification with the soul of a sport – for the people 'who know the difference between winning and achieving grace.'

Creative Director, Hal Arneson says:

> We have our songlines[2] – they're passed on and they're very seldom written down. They run through generations and they extend out into the customer base. We definitely include our customers as part of that tribal culture. The mythology of the company expands.

Patagonia is not afraid to involve its customers in what it does. One of the contradictions is that the output of the company is the production of expensive garments largely made from carbon-based, non-renewable petrochemicals, which take thousands of years to degrade. Rather than trying to rationalize this dilemma internally, the company raised the issue on the Web and asked people what it should do. A cynical attempt to build support for an impossible situation or a genuine desire to involve its customers? The history of Patagonia would suggest the latter. However, whatever the motivation, the request generated a lot of comment and helped the company to decide that the only solution was to build clothing of the highest quality while causing the least possible harm in doing so. The view was that the better the quality, the longer the garment would last. Instead of a one-year fashion purchase a product should have a ten-year plus life.

In 1996, nearly 40 years after Yvon Chouinard first started black-smithing, the company decided it should formally articulate its overall purpose and values. This wasn't about creating something new, but was about drawing out and defining the philosophy that had long steered people's behaviour. A cross-functional group of some 30 people talked about the company and its beliefs and came to the following definition.

Our purpose (where we mean to take the company):

To use business to inspire and implement solutions to the environmental crisis.

Our core values (the characteristics that define the company):

Quality: pursuit of ever-greater quality in everything we do.

Integrity: relationships built on integrity and respect.

Environmentalism: serve as a catalyst for personal and corporate action.

Not bound by convention: our success – and much of the fun – lies in developing innovative ways to do things.

Typically for Patagonia the purpose and values were given context by writing a 28-page book called *Defining Quality*, which talks through the history of the company and recounts the seminal moments in its development. As suggested in the purpose statement, environmental concerns loom large in Patagonia's thinking. Of course, there are other organizations such as The Body Shop, Ben & Jerry's and The Cooperative Bank that have pursued overt environmental or ethical strategies. All have been criticized by different parties for the legitimacy of their stances. For example, The Cooperative Bank was criticized by Balmer and Wilkinson[3] for making ethical claims that did not correlate with the reality of the bank's area of activity. However, the main area of distrust is that environmentalism is often used as a marketing tool to create a point of distinctiveness, rather than something that is a genuine principle. For Patagonia, environmentalism has long been part of the lifeblood of the company and, given the nature of the company's products, something that Patagonia's people encounter in a very direct way. The benefit to Patagonia is not so much in the marketing of products, as Patagonia feels uncomfortable with the very idea. Chris van Dyke, who joined Patagonia from Nike says:

When I joined, Yvon was very anti-marketing, but I presented marketing to him as a way of relationship building; a way of creating a friendship…the great thing is it's a culture that is so rich in stories.

The real value of environmentalism in an organizational sense is that it is the glue that binds the organization. It engages the people who work for the company and it is a clear aid to decision making, such that when both tactical and strategic decisions have to be made there is a clear reference point. People simply have to ask themselves: 'are we being true to the brand?' The more precise the brand idea the easier it is to use it as a means of accountability. In particular, the greater the authenticity of the brand the easier it will be for the organization to be consistent, especially when confronting adversity. For example, the Patagonia catalogue is always printed on chlorine free and recycled paper. Yet, when the paper for the summer 2000 catalogue arrived at the printer it was an unusable batch. There were only two possible alternatives available for such a large print run. One was a paper that passed the environmental standards that Patagonia set, but was poor for reproducing photographs. The other paper contained chlorine and was not recycled, but was a high-quality material that was very good for reproducing images. When the problem was discussed, everyone agreed that going for the inferior paper would lose sales but that the high quality paper would undermine the integrity of the company. The choice to accept lost sales was apparently an easy one.

One might imagine that the environmental emphasis is constraining. It certainly cuts out certain activities but it also provides a focus for innovation. As the explicit purpose of Patagonia has permeated the whole business, so the company's commitment to environmentalism has been extended. The company now gives away 1 per cent of sales revenue to non-profit groups, mostly locally based environmental bodies; it has converted the company's cotton products to organic even though production costs went up 25 per cent and sales went down 20 per cent; it trains people in non-violent civil disobedience and posts bail for those arrested; it provides employees with time off to work for an environmental group and it works with its suppliers and other companies, such as Dow Chemicals, to reduce environmental impacts.

Chip is the brand

The clarity of the Patagonia brand would count for little if it remained the preserve of Yvon Chouinard and his senior managers.

However its real power is the way in which it seems to permeate the organization. In this sense Chip is an exemplar of the brand and all that it stands for. The choice to investigate Patagonia as a brand for this book was based largely on two initial interactions: purchasing and being impressed by the quality of the products and reading the organizational stories. Patagonia's distinctive business model and its search for a principled approach make for intriguing reading. However, it was visiting Patagonia's offices in California that was most persuasive and, as a testament to word-of-mouth communication, it is a story I have since told anecdotally to individuals and in presentations. When I contacted the PR Director Lu Setnicka and asked how to get to the offices, she described the directions and then said go into the building and meet Chip. I thought it strange that I should be given the name of the receptionist. Chip was sitting in the entrance next to a noticeboard with a chalked 'welcome to Nicholas Ind', alongside the latest surfing report. Chip stood up smiled, shook my hand, introduced himself and welcomed me to Patagonia. If I wanted a coffee or any refreshments he suggested I go and help myself in the staff canteen. Then, as I sat in reception, Chip answered the phone and greeted new visitors in the same way he had me, stopping to chat about the surfing and Patagonia, if he had time between calls. What struck me was that he was perfectly natural with everyone he met. If he could convey that attitude to the approximately 1,500 phone calls he received every day and to the stream of visitors to the offices, Chip would be a vital component in Patagonia's image. Afterwards, when I thought of all the office receptions I've been into in the last 20 years, I couldn't recall anyone as positive as Chip. The question that intrigued me afterwards was why? Sitting on reception must involve a high level of repetition. So, to find the answer I spoke to Chip again and asked him whether he had been told to behave in a certain way. Were there rules or did he just do what he thought appropriate? This is Chip's reply:

> I ride my bike to work everyday, some of my children come to the childcare programme here. It seemed that when I arrived at work not only was I in a good mood, it was easy to work with our customers and our guests. It's an image that comes naturally – standing up, shaking hands, smiling. I'm genuinely feeling groovy. It's seamless for me to give customer

service and interact with people and to give them a feeling that it is a different place; that it is a business where you can be yourself – caring and giving top-notch customer service. It's easy for me.

Every store whether you're in Atlanta or New York or Ventura or whether you call over the phone in Reno, the people at the other end are focused on customer service. It's a fun, outdoor company. It's easy for a retail sales associate to give customer service, because for the most part they just got back from a great trip and they did something exciting and they're able to convey not only the good times but the gear to wear, the products to use. They have first-hand experience of a lot of the sports.

I answer most of the calls, although I have wonderful back-up staff. The company is flexible if I want to go on a long vacation or just have a day off to be with my children.

I encompass every value of the company. We have speakers in to talk about the environment and you also see there's no compromise on quality. It's so neat to be involved with those things. It reinforces my integrity as an employee and as a person. We're not bound by convention.

I'm 11 times world Frisbee champion. I do surfing and I've developed a surf class so I teach surfing to employees and also private lessons. I'm responsible for putting the surf report up on the board – we have people all over Ventura County telling us what the surf is like.

My reactions come naturally from absorbing all of our values – environment, integrity, quality – all of that is relayed back out when I'm on the phone. When I'm on the phone, I want to know what the person at the other end is going to feel; what the picture is in their mind. It's the image they have of Patagonia that equals a strong brand.

The best bit is working with our customers and working with our vendors; being the image and the voice of Patagonia. I think my job is one of the most important in the company and I'm well respected within our community of employees.

Everybody respects me. I feel special and I take my job seriously and I love every aspect of it.

In Patagonia

In 1968, when Yvon Chouinard should have been making pitons, he chose instead to drive a van with some climbing friends south from California through Central and South America to Patagonia. Chouinard fell in love with this elemental place and its fjords, glaciers and mountains; where the winds blow powerfully for six months of the year (the writer and aviator, Antoine de Saint-Exupéry, found his plane flew backward instead of forward in Patagonia). It is also isolated and inspiring: 'travellers from Darwin onwards noted how this bleakness seized the imagination.'[4] When, a few years later, Chouinard moved into outdoor clothing, he named the new company after the region. It was an apt metaphor for Chouinard's company. Not only did it represent, in a practical sense, the type of location where Patagonia's clothing was designed to be functionally effective, it also stood for the imagination that is at the heart of the Patagonia brand. Commentators often talk about brands as experiences – and Patagonia is certainly that – but this brand is more profoundly about imagination. Read *Patagonia's Notes from the Field* – a collection of customer and employee stories from the Patagonia catalogue – and you are transported to high peaks, frozen waters and running rivers. You imagine yourself riding a wave, climbing a rock face, or wandering through a desert. Although there is an element of New Ageism in some of Patagonia's ideas, they undoubtedly capture the imagination. The brand, from Chip to the advertising to the products, encourages dreams. For employees too, there is the opportunity to dream; to imagine different ways of doing things. Partly this is to do with the blurring of the boundaries between the outside of the organization and the inside – a small but apposite example of this is the way I was invited by Chip to help myself to food and drink in the staff canteen. The employees of the company are also the consumers of the environmental vision, the company's products and its advertising. An employee can be the same person outside of the organization and inside. This enables the creative department to develop marketing communications that derive from the imagination of both customers and employees. This union is the central tenet in the authenticity of Patagonia. As Hal Arneson says:

> Most of the people here are risk athletes. They're outdoor people working in an indoor environment that allows them to work here because it respects that about them. People are passionate about their sports and they bring that into the workplace. People spend time here agonizing over whether what they do has meaning.

The freedom to use imagination might be seen by many organizations as a licence for organizational anarchy. The value of tapping into the collective imagination and ideas of an organization could be outweighed by the difficulty of maintaining focus. This is where articulating and embedding the organization's purpose and values creates real benefits. Employees can be 'unbound by convention' if there is clarity about what the values mean. Take, for example, the idea of quality. This is an overused word in value statements, but Patagonia has a clear idea of what it means by it. Patagonia's view of quality is 'specific and opinionated' and based on:

- fulfilling a functional need (otherwise the product shouldn't exist);
- paring a product down to its essence;
- tested performance;
- durability;
- environmental responsibility.

The importance of specificity is that quality moves from being a vague idea to something that has a real impact on organizational decision making. It means that the materials used are effective, the design is driven by the function of the product and the testing procedures are robust, if not extreme. One can see the hand of Yvon Chouinard in this thinking. Nothing has really changed from the early days of piton making, which is perhaps why customers and employees not only trust Patagonia but are powerful advocates of the brand.

Summary

Yvon Chouinard would be described by some as an idealist – in the derogatory sense of the word. However, Chouinard's idealism, which seems shared in large measure by the employees and loyal customers of Patagonia, has created a brand that has sincerity and authenticity. The company does not try to appeal to everyone and the potential for identification that this nurtures helps to create a strong bond. For risk athletes and environmentalists it provides the opportunity to find meaning through work, which is perhaps part of the reason why the company has been listed for three consecutive years (1998, 1999, 2000) in Fortune's 100 best companies to work for in America.[5] Others might argue that the Patagonia model is only sustainable for a private company. Certainly, Nike (who were also interviewed for this book) in its early days, exhibited many of the same Robin Hood, anti-establishment characteristics of Patagonia – something it found harder to sustain as it grew and became a publicly quoted company with a new set of audiences. Now that Patagonia has made a clear commitment to growth, the task will be to maintain its principles as it gets larger. Will compromises have to be made? Will Patagonia be able to keep its close relationship with customers when its circle of friends widens? We should hope that Patagonia manages these potential contradictions. We need mavericks who question the way things are done; who wear their principles on their sleeves; who truly fulfil employees' working lives.

The story of Patagonia is the opening chapter in this book because it demonstrates many of the themes that will be explored in subsequent chapters. Specifically, it suggests:

- employees flourish in organizations where they identify with the brand;
- organizations flourish when the brand has relevance and creates meaning;
- purpose and values are not created – they exist; the issue is how well they are articulated and embedded;

- brand clarity creates freedom;
- brands come to life when the boundaries between the internal and external blur;
- stories and myths are important for sustaining brands;
- living the brand requires imagination.

Notes

1 Gallagher, Nora (ed) (1999) *Patagonia – Notes from the Field*, Chronicle Books, San Francisco, p 63.
2 A songline is an Aboriginal concept that was popularized by the writer Bruce Chatwin in his book *The Songlines*. It is an inner guide, which forms the basis of an Aborigine's spiritual life. An outsider cannot understand its truth.
3 Wilkinson, A and Balmer, JMT (1996) Corporate and Generic Identities: lessons from the Cooperative Bank, *International Journal of Bank Marketing*, 14 (4), pp 22–35.
4 Shakespeare, N (2000) *Bruce Chatwin*, Vintage, p 289.
5 The Fortune 100 best is employee driven with two-thirds of the scoring based on answers employees give to 57 questions on the Great Place to Work Index Trust. In 2000, 33,457 randomly selected employees filled out the survey. The other third is based on an evaluation of corporate responses to the Great Place to Work Culture Audit and a human resources questionnaire.

two

Living **brands**

Following on from the specific example of Patagonia, this chapter will investigate the nature of branding and the important role that employees play in brand formation. Although the primary emphasis here will be on businesses, voluntary organizations and governmental organizations can also be seen as brands – although they sometimes feel uncomfortable with the word, associated as it is with consumerism. Even politicians are sometimes talked about as brands but I am not sure the extension of the idea is truly credible.

The primary function of brands is to reduce our anxiety in making choices. The very fact we are anxious indicates that we have freedom to choose. The more we sense we know about a product, the less anxiety we feel. When we know less about a product, then our uncertainty rises. This axiom is demonstrated by the correlation that exists between familiarity and favourability. We would tend to trust an established car brand such as BMW or Mercedes, more than a car brand we have never heard of. The more we think we know, the more comfortable we are. However, this is not a purely rational process where we can quantify the specific benefits. Much of the time we are making guesses based on imperfect information and on a range of rational and emotional factors. For example, choosing to donate money to WWF rather than Amnesty International or Save the Children is a mixture of the emotional, the rational and the comparative. In this instance we will identify with the cause, as we understand it, believe in the benefits our money can deliver and make a mental comparison of the relative impact of the different organizations. We will not conduct a cost benefit analysis, which leads to the 'right' decision. Rather, we rely on the brand idea as a proxy. The organization – through its reported activities, communications and employee behaviour – provides us with an approximation of the organizational reality. Then, if the signals we receive are proven by experience, our anxiety is reduced in subsequent interactions and we may come to trust the brand and even become advocates for it. The only danger with reducing anxiety and taking the risk out of the things we do and buy is that we can become bored.[1] As we become ever more confident as consumers – a fact long observed by the Henley Centre for Forecasting – we sometimes yearn for adventure and for novelty; for actively experiencing anxiety. This willingness, which varies from individual to individual, leads to a consequent reduction in consumer loyalty. People are more willing to experiment with different products and with different channels of delivery, such as shopping on the Web. To meet this need the brand needs to balance continuity of experience with innovation – to provide unpredictability within a framework of predictable values. Think back for a moment to the constant innovation of Patagonia. There are always new products in the range, but they always conform to the organization's ideas of integrity, environmentalism and quality. Values are the defining guide for the brand.

Defining brands

In the marketing arena, there are almost as many definitions of branding as there are books on the subject. I do not intend to add to the confusion. The definition I have found to work best comes from advertising planner, Paul Feldwick, who says 'At its simplest, a brand is a recognisable and trustworthy badge of origin and also a promise of performance.'[2]

Feldwick goes on to point out that brands also transform experiences and provide a means of differentiation. Many of the ideas about branding, however, Feldwick's included, are derived largely from manufactured goods, whereas increasingly we work in and consume services rather than products. This means that although the definition holds up, the implications extend beyond it.

A badge of origin

Organizations spend large sums of money generating names, developing visual identities and designing packaging, all of which can be a valuable means of signifying what to expect from an organization. We buy the Nike Swoosh as opposed to the Adidas Triple Stripe, or vice versa, because we have an idea of what to expect, derived from advertising, from the styling and from endorsements. We have a mental picture of the brand and what it might say about us. Nonetheless, we should not mistake the sign for the substance. The swoosh sets up the expectation, but if the product fails to deliver, we will begin to change our perceptions of the badge of origin. A similar situation occurs with a service-based brand or a corporate brand, where there are multiple audiences. The British Airways badge of origin comprising primarily the name, the ribbon and the multi-cultural tail fins encourages us to believe in the company as a professional and truly global brand. However, the trust in that badge can easily be undermined by encounters with cabin or ground crew. Consequently brands are not easy to manage.

Companies often communicate their brand messages through a variety of conduits. Just think of a brand you know well and consider how you form your opinion of it. The process is multi-faceted. It is about the interactions with people, what you read in the press, the ease of use and content on the Web site, the style of the advertising, the quality of the product and the efficiency of the after-sales service. The company may try to control all of these outputs, but it is only the visual presentation that is truly policeable. Content is not. Even in the tightest structures you cannot create an Orwellian world where every employee thinks and talks in the same way. Nor would it be desirable to do so. The power of a brand lies in giving employees the freedom to use their imaginations within the constraints set by the organization's values. So the badge is just a badge. If the design of the badge is good then it can help an organization stand out from its competitors and indicate its provenance. But the badge is not the brand. In fact the truism is that the brand exists in the minds of stakeholders – they, rather than the company, determine the nature of the brand relationship. The inference is that although the company intends to communicate an idea of brand through its signs and symbols, there is no guarantee that consumers and other audiences will read them in the intended way.[3] People cannot help using their different personal and cultural experiences to decipher what they see.

A promise of performance

A promise is implicit in a brand. From the combination of corporate messages and experience we believe that we will receive a certain experience from a brand. The Patagonia name on a garment promises me quality and environmental responsibility. It also has a transformational quality, as observed in the last chapter, in that it captures my imagination and conjures up pictures of skiing or climbing. It also makes me feel more professional and adventurous because I associate the product with the experienced sports people I see wearing the clothes, the knowledgeable staff in the stores and the images in the catalogue. Whether the promise of performance is delivered or not defines my evolving relationship with the brand. If each interaction – whether it is through products or people or communications – confirms my idea about the brand, then the relationship gets stronger. This is why there needs to be a tonal consistency to the brand; that the experiences I have support each other. This does not suggest that each interaction carries the same weight. A media commentary in a respected journal might have a greater, or at least different, influence than an advertisement. A leaked document might have a greater legitimacy than the annual report. What we are seeking to establish is the authenticity of the brand. Can it be trusted? Insights gained from objective third parties or from unguarded comments undesigned for general consumption can enable us to see behind the brand façade; to discover the truth. This is a journey of deconstruction. As consumers, or indeed citizens, we have become more cynical and less trusting. Generally we don't believe what politicians tell us, nor do we have much faith in the press or business.[4] In a consumer context this lack of faith has spawned organizations, like the Consumers' Association and JD Power, which survey products and services and provide us with more objective evaluations of brands. Similarly, there are large numbers of Web communities that provide forums for discussing the truth about brands. If you want to buy a new product you can read reviews, do research, discuss user experiences and publish your own views – all on the Web, at no cost to you, except in time. This is a medium that makes it very hard for companies to hide their failings. When consumers start seeing inconsistency, they start questioning. For example, if the Patagonia receptionist had been rude and aggressive, I might have started to question the brand; to wonder whether the company is well managed and takes care of its staff.

There seems little point in spending large sums promoting an idealized picture of a brand through advertising, if the brand itself cannot deliver. This seemingly simple premiss is ignored with surprising regularity. A case in point is the start-up online sportswear retailer Boo.com, which spent $135 million in a year, much of it on advertising, without ever resolving content and technology on its Web site or providing adequate logistics. Other examples are those airlines, some of which have spent up to $80 million on creating and then applying visual identities and then undermining the expenditure through unhelpful staff. This, despite the fact that it has been shown through empirical studies of airlines that the experience with personnel and cabin crew in particular is a prime determinant of customer satisfaction.

Sometimes airlines become indignant about criticism and argue that most of what they do is well thought out and executed and that it is only a small percentage of occasions when there are problems which get amplified. Take for example the US diplomat, George Howard, who seems to have been thwarted at every turn in his attempts to fly home to the United States, following a bereavement in his family. Such was his frustration that he published his letter for all to read on the Web[5].

TO: BRITISH AIRWAYS
ATTN: CUSTOMER SERVICE
SUBJECT: COMPLAINT
FROM: George Howard, U S Diplomat, US EMBASSY KUWAIT
PO Box 24
APO AE – 09880–9000

I am writing this letter in reference to a devastating and horrible experience I had with BRITISH AIRWAYS.

On the morning of 24 March 1999 I received a Red Cross message that there had been a death in my family and my presence was needed. The US Embassy immediately began coordinating my travel arrangements. AL-Rashed International travel was working with BRITISH AIRWAYS to get a confirmed reservation. At 5pm on the 24th of March I was informed that I had a confirmed reservation on British Airways Flt 156 @ 0150 25 March 99. I purchased the ticket for $1,830.00 and showed up at the airport three (3) hours prior to departure. I immediately noticed the British Airways Agents were very disorganized. Mr. Sharif, British Airways Agent took my ticket and passport gave it to another agent and walked away. I waited and watched the agents pass around my documents for 1½ hours and nothing was being done. I continuously asked what the problem was and why I wasn't being checked in and was given no definite answers. During this period of time I observed other passengers being checked in with no problem. After more time passed I was finally told that the flight was overbooked and I would not be able to make this flight. I explained about the death in my family and the information was in the computer. I stressed that I really needed to make this flight. I was told that my emergency situation was of no concern to British Airways and would have [to] wait until the next day to get a flight. I remained at the airport until 3am trying to get something definite from British Airways agents. I was finally told that I would be on the next day's flight and all connections and flight numbers would be the same.

On the next day, I again arrived three (3) hours ahead of departure time. British Airlines was just as disorganized as the night before and didn't seem to know what to do with my ticket. After approximately an hour I was told that I could make the flight and all times and places for connections would be the same as the day before. After arriving at Heathrow Airport London I went to the United Airlines counter to check in for my flight to Chicago on Flt. # 939. I was told by agent Dominic Falleiro that I did not have a reservation on Flight #939 to Chicago. I explained that British Airways had made the reservations and confirmation for this flight. I also showed him my baggage checks that showed the route my bags were going which corresponded to the ticket I was holding. I suggested that he call British Airways and try to find out what had happened. He refused to make any inquiries to British Airways until I insisted that he do so. I accompanied him to the British Airways counter where I was told once again that I had no reservation and would have to wait until they did some checking to find out what had happened. After about an hour Ms. Jane Young (British Airways Agent) told me that it appeared that a reservation had been made by their airlines with United, but it had been cancelled and she was confused about why since my bags had been checked through. Ms Young told me she would have to do another ticket but it would have to be through the Gatwick airport which was 1 hour away by bus. She said I would first have to go to the baggage area to get my bags, claim them, go through customs and then catch the bus to Gatwick. It was 9:15am and the flight from Gatwick would leave at 11:00am. Another British Airways agent, who was supposedly assisting Ms. Young by the name of Julia Chistodoulou made a statement upon hearing about my flight being due to a death in the family that 'as long as you get there in the end Mr. Howard, that is all that matters'. As a customer service agent, I think this was a very insensitive remark that showed no concern on the part of British Airways as to whether a person has an emergency or whether they arrive at their destination on time.

After completing the tasks which had been told me by Ms Young, and certainly without any assistance from British Airways personnel, I arrived at the bus departure only to be told that the bus was broken down. I had to wait another 15 minutes in very cold and rain for another bus which when it did arrive had a broken heater. I arrived at Gatwick airport 15 minutes before Flt 2289 to Phoenix departed. I again attempted to check in and was told I had no reservation. Once again I explained my situation to the agent. She tried to sort out the problem realizing that she only had 15 minutes prior to departure, but to no avail. She then told me to go to the aircraft, which was some distance away (Gate #63), and try to board while she continued to sort things out. My nightmare didn't end because upon trying to board I was told that I had no seat and to stand in the Jetway until something could be done. Even though I was totally stressed out by this time, I stood in the cold Jetway and waited. Finally I did get a seat and departed for Phoenix on Flt # 2289. Upon arriving in Phoenix I attempted to check in on America West Flt. 2290 (America West) to San Jose, Ca. And was again told I did not have a reservation. This required another explanation to another agent and total frustration on my part while this agent went through the sorting out process and finally got me on my flight.

Upon returning to Kuwait I was informed by the US Embassy Travel Office that the manager of the British Airways office had called them and complained that after going out of their way to get me a confirmed reservation on the 25th of March, I VOLUNTEERED to take a later flight and it didn't appear that I had an emergency. I immediately went to the British Airways office to set the record straight and spoke to Ms. Sonia Ashlan. She checked the records and found that in fact I had been offloaded against my will and it was documented that I had an emergency. This was a case of the manager trying to cover up the irresponsible conduct on behalf of British Airways and the extent they will go to make the consumer look bad.

I have heard that the average person comes in contact with at least 75 people every month and bad news travels fast. When anyone asks me about my worst travel experience in my twenty five (25) years of frequent traveling, I would have to say my British Airlines flight from Kuwait to San Jose, Ca. I sincerely hope that no one else has to experience this type of treatment, especially during a time of bereavement. I also hope that you take my letter seriously and make the series of problems that I experienced the exception and not the rule when traveling with British Airways. I have been left with the bitter taste in my mouth that I was at the mercy of an airline that has no focus on quality or customer service…only the bottom line…Profits!

Sincerely, George Howard

As consumers, we can be forgiving of a brand, especially if most of the experiences we have are positive, but sometimes the one experience we have is very bad and we then infer the general from the particular. As the writer Iris Murdoch notes:

> We see parts of things, we intuit whole things. We seem to know a great deal on the basis of very little…we fear plurality, diffusion, senseless accident, chaos, we want to transform what we cannot dominate or understand into something reassuring and familiar.[6]

A point of difference

When we choose to buy a product or a service, both positive and negative reasoning influences us. The degree of consideration given will depend on the complexity and the size of the purchase but the factors will tend to be similar. The first factor is functionality. Does the product do what I need it to do? The second is 'does it appeal to me emotionally? Does the product tap into my needs and desires and sense of self?' The third is differentiation. 'What is the context for this product and how is it different from the other products that I could substitute for it?' In a sense, 'what is it not?' Strong brands tend to be opinionated. They clearly stand for something and provide a positive reason for choice. Many brands do not have this clarity. Partly this is because genuine product innovation has become more difficult. A technical innovation, unless it has the protection of patents, is often easily replicable, while stylistic innovation tends to bring plagiarists in its wake. Think of the Apple iMac and its use of colour and plastics and those who imitated it, or the Dyson vacuum cleaner and its imitators. Services are even easier to copy. For example, a new financial product is easily replicable. The problem is the time lag required structuring the product and developing the necessary promotional material. In the Internet world each market has multiple competitors that offer broadly similar services. Just key 'pets' into a search engine and see how many sites come up, all offering broadly similar concepts. If the choice of site is to be anything other than serendipity, then there needs to be a relevant point of difference.

In the words of Apple Computer, organizations need to 'think different'. That requires them to keep giving people new reasons to choose them. Innovation of itself is not enough. Innovation has to be focused on delivering functional and emotional benefits to consumers. The brand is thus a combination of interactions that collectively differentiate the brand. As Stephen King in *Developing New Brands* says: 'A product is something that is made in a factory; a brand is something that is bought, by a customer. A product can be copied by a competitor; a brand is unique.'[7]

Corporate brands

Branding is more complex at the corporate level. The organization not only has to manage its relationship with consumers – it has to take into account all the other stakeholders such as investors, media, government, suppliers, buyers and employees. Each of these will have a different expectation and understanding of the brand. Investors will be interested in strategy and performance whereas customers will be interested in price and product quality. Each audience will be working to deconstruct the organization but they will often be searching for different things. What unites them is a common interest in 'seeing backstage' – seeing the people behind the brand. This opening up to the world can be a daunting prospect for businesses. In the past there was security in erecting barriers between the organization and its stakeholders. This has become far harder to sustain. Partly this is because, if organizations are to gain competitive advantage, they need to interact with and learn from their stakeholders. Ideas need to be shared and knowledge needs to be acquired. As *The Cluetrain Manifesto* says 'Not only do your customers want to talk with real people inside your organisation, but your employees are desperate to talk with real customers. They want to tell them the truth.'[8]

Partly it is because the near universal access to the Web makes the barriers themselves permeable. 'Challenge is in the air because the digital world removes the emperor's clothes. It makes Bill Clinton transparent, GE transparent, the UN transparent. And, you, too are transparent.'[9]

The organization therefore needs to structure its brand to meet this transparency. It cannot make claims without substantive evidence and it cannot engage in wishful thinking about its status in or influence upon people's lives. Figure 2.1 below conveys two key concepts in this regard: the image that consumers have of a brand cannot be controlled in any absolute sense – several different elements impact on consumer perceptions – and many of the impacts are outside of the organization's structure.

Consumers interested in buying a specific computer brand will perhaps be influenced by advertising, press reviews, interaction with employees, their overall perceptions of computer manufacturers, other owners of this computer (virtual and actual word of mouth), software manufacturers and retailers. The computer manufacturer may make an excellent product, but the actions of partners, retailers and other manufacturers could all have negative impacts. As services

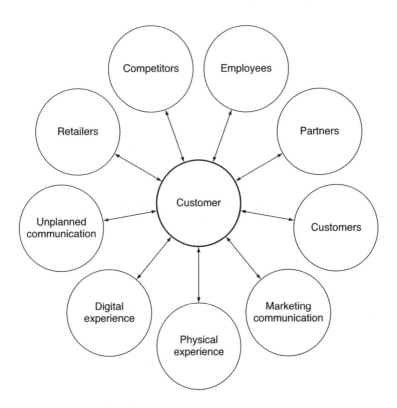

Figure 2.1 Networked brands

and products are increasingly delivered by networked organizations, there is potential for others to either add to the perception of the value of the brand or to detract from it. As with employees, partners and other brand participants need to be engaged with the idea of the brand in a genuine way. Often there are simply too many people involved in the formation of the brand image for anything but authenticity to be valid. Consistency of communication can only be achieved if the brand idea is credible and comprehensible. As a result we may start to see a more authentic, less exaggerated language entering the realm of brandspeak.

Another corollary of this brand transparency is that although stakeholders seek different information there are increased possibilities for overlap. Information on the Web that is aimed at shareholders will be readily accessible to employees, and consumer information can readily be scrutinized in unforeseen ways by an investor. This requires organizations to ensure consistency of communication, which is not always easy to achieve in a fragmented structure, where different departments are talking to these audiences. This situation is exacerbated in organizations with multiple Web sites for different geographic areas or divisions. The best way of resolving these forces is through clarity.

People

There is a tendency to talk about brands in an abstract way. They are seen as things that have value. Coca-Cola is worth $72.5 billion, Microsoft $70.2 billion, IBM $53.2 billion, Intel $39 billion and Nokia $38.5 billion.[10] However, brands are created and consumed by people. The managers of a business formulate strategies, communications people write briefs and help develop advertising and design programmes, sales people build relationships with customers, industrial designers create new products and receptionists greet people. Consumers are not target markets devoid of any persona; they are individuals, some of whom act in similar ways when encountering a brand. The relationship between employees and consumers is therefore at the heart of the brand experience. Just as in any successful relationship, the employee/consumer relationship needs honesty, openness and a unity of interest. Where the unity is intuitive, with employees and consumers sharing the same passions, it is particularly powerful. This factor helped to create a powerful brand for both Nike and Patagonia.

In traditional marketing and advertising thinking, communications people would talk about owning the relationship with consumers. This is fundamentally flawed. The prime mover in the relationship is the consumer, not the marketing department or the advertising agency. Even within the organization, the relationship with the consumer is one that the whole enterprise must embrace, otherwise it does not have a relationship; it has one-way communication, much of which is probably ill-targeted and consequently wasted. For the organization to move to a stance where the consumer is the focus of its attention does not require archery target charts with the word 'consumer' in the middle. It necessitates an orientation where everyone thinks and acts like the consumer. This humanistic approach seems to have been lost in the often-militaristic jargon of business and the abstraction that stems from ever-larger organizations.

However, there are important opportunities for change. Some organizations, such as the Swedish-Swiss ABB and Swedish Internet consultancy Framfab, build cells that are never allowed to grow too large. This small scale keeps the business focused on customers; they don't become abstractions. Equally, the Web has shown what businesses should know intuitively: that customers have the real power. Some of the most interesting Web businesses are demand driven. Consumers tell suppliers what they will pay. For example, priceline.com lets customers bid for cars, flights and hotels, by offering what they want. The price is up to the consumer. Similarly, letsbuyit.com aggregates customer demand to push prices down. At the corporate level there are hundreds of Web trading markets where, instead of companies selling to buyers in a traditional way, there is an exchange, where buyer and seller meet electronically. And then there are services where consumers have subverted the accepted ways of doing things. Linus Torvald's creation, Linux is an operating software that is available free over the Web and because he made the source code open, is subject to continual enhancements by its devoted band of followers. Nearly a third of Web servers now use Linux.

Summary

Brands should be both a source of differentiation and a promise of performance. The presentation of the brand is an element in the way customers see a brand, but it is not the brand itself. Rather, a brand is something that exists in people's minds. The company may seek to influence that mental image but success can be only relative. Planned and unplanned communications are received all the time and consequently the brand is a loose collation of fact and myth.

The best way to develop a brand that has a high degree of relevance and consistency is to ensure that the employees of an organization understand and believe in the values of the organization. These cannot be invented – they have to come from the essence of the organization. However, they do have to be lived sincerely if they are to meet the deconstructivist gaze of consumers and other audiences. Living brands have to be built on solid ground but they also have to be capable of evolution and change.

Notes

1 Read Anne Tyler's book *The Accidental Tourist* (Vintage, 1995) for an example of a risk-free life. The central character writes travel guides for Americans who would rather not travel. The purpose of the guides is to insulate people against risk. For example, he advises travellers always to have a good book with them so that they don't have to talk to the person next to them on the plane. Similarly, the restaurants he recommends in Paris are all American.
2 Feldwick, P (1991) Defining a Brand, in *Understanding Brands*, ed D Cowley, Kogan Page, London, p21.
3 The American pragmatist philosopher, CS Peirce has argued that one combination of signs has to be interpreted by another set. Thus when we see a logo or brand name, we use a set of linguistic ideas, such as caring, reputable, exciting. Not only is there no guarantee that the next person will use the same linguistic ideas, but also is there no certainty that they would mean the same things by them, even if they did use the same ideas.

4 The Henley Centre for Forecasting and Gallup's research into faith in institutions in Britain shows dramatic falls in confidence of all institutions. Most notable is the fact that public confidence in Parliament fell from 54 per cent in 1983 to just 9 per cent in 1995. The research is supported by work done by MORI, which shows that only 11 per cent of people trust what government Ministers have to say. MORI also found that, when they asked people why companies support society and the community, 64 per cent said that it was to cover up anti-social activities.

5 The transcript of this letter can be found on the Web at www.aviation-uk.com/diplomat.htm

6 Murdoch, Iris (1992) *Metaphysics as a Guide to Morals*, Penguin, Harmondsworth.

7 King, Stephen (1984) *Developing New Brands*, JWT, London, p iii.

8 Levine, Rick et al (1999) *The Cluetrain Manifesto*, Perseus Books, Cambridge, MA, p 94.

9 Ridderstråle, Jonas and Nordstrom, Kjell (2000) *Funky Business*, p 46.

10 Interbrand brand valuations – published July 2000.

three

Why **people need vision and values**

'There is now, more than ever, some need for Utopia, in the sense that men need – as they have always needed – some vision of their potential, some manner of fusing passion with intelligence.'

So wrote Daniel Bell, some 50 years ago in *The End of Ideology*. He was proclaiming, as Francis Fukuyama did later in his essay, 'The End of History', that the central rivalry between the political left and right was over. Bell's view was that, even if political ideas were dead, people need an outlet for their passions and their intellect. That outlet can be, and indeed should be, the world of work. Brands can come to life if organizations engage with people's deeper needs and if they help to fill the vacuum that has emerged within the lives of many. However, to achieve this, business leaders need to understand what motivates employees to join a business, what makes them stay and what encourages them to identify with organizational goals. Armed with this understanding, organizations can build people-centred businesses where the full intellectual capacity of individuals is used. Rather than employees who are represented in body but not spirit, you can create 'brand evangelists': people who believe and will preach for the organization.

Why go to work

As Abraham Maslow pointed out in his famous hierarchy of needs, we work because we have basic needs of safety and security. For anyone who has spent time unemployed or has felt uncertain about their position within an organization, there is a real fear of not being able to afford the necessities of life: clothing oneself properly, eating well enough and caring for one's family.

These basic needs are formidable drivers, but they do not of themselves encourage people to identify with organizations or create what Bartlett and Ghosal refer to as, 'the extraordinary effort and sustained commitment required to deliver consistently superior performance.'[1] However, the safety-and-security view of life and indeed work prevailed for the first half of the 20th century and it led to ideas of scientific management: that people were simply cogs in the production process and could be ordered and managed. If they met the requirements they would be rewarded for their output. If they did not they were discarded. Not surprisingly, this helped to create uncertainty and adversarial relationships between management and workers. Management would try to extract the maximum production for the least payment and workers and their unions would try to negotiate the maximum payment for their efforts. There was little sense of a commonly pursued agenda. As recently as 1983, Kenichi Ohmae observed in

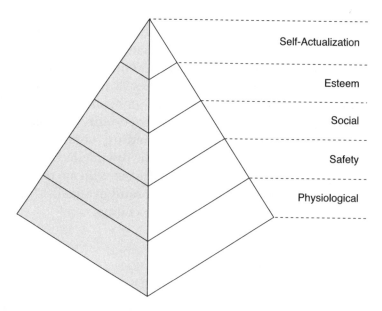

Figure 3.1 Maslow's Hierarchy of Needs

the best-selling book *The Mind of the Strategist* that the Japanese had a distinctive viewpoint in that workers and management shared a consistent perspective on corporate goals. His inference was that managers and employees in the rest of the world did not.

Maslow, with his belief in humanistic psychology recognized that, although people do have basic needs, they also have social needs, and needs for self-esteem and self-actualization. He believed that each person's task is to be the best person they can. Not everyone can become an astronaut or US President or head of a multinational organization, but they can make the most of their individual potential. Most people do want to build relationships; they do want to be recognized by others for their worth and they do want a sense of fulfilment.

Self-actualization

A musician must make music, an artist must paint, a poet must write, if he is to be ultimately at peace with himself. What a man can be, he must be. This need we may call self actualisation...It refers to man's desire for self-fulfilment, namely to the tendency for him to become actually in what he is potentially: to become everything that one is capable of becoming.[2]

Of course the reality of the world is that not everyone does achieve his or her potential. Some people underachieve. Yet Maslow would argue that they do not do so willingly. Even when people fail, they still have the desire to achieve – to 'experience higher values'. This can be seen in those charities that work with disadvantaged youth. In the United Kingdom, with its problems of youth unemployment, teenage pregnancies, drug abuse and crime, there is a periodic hand wringing about the underachievement of Britain's teenagers. However, one of the charities – Fairbridge – which works with the most difficult cases, has a workforce of which 30 per cent are these supposed no hope-teenagers. They employ them not as an act of charity but because these are people who are best able to relate to other young people. Others go on to employment and higher education. Yet, when these teenagers first arrive at Fairbridge they are sometimes third-generation unemployed, unable to read and write properly and incapable of communication. How is this transformation achieved? First, the organization is non-judgmental – anyone is welcome. Second, it provides a supportive environment and mentoring. Third, it encourages people to set their own objectives in life – and to then take a series of small steps to achieve them. Lastly, they celebrate their successes. What Fairbridge gives these disadvantaged teenagers is confidence and the motivation to succeed in what they choose to do. The teenagers do the rest. It is an example of the innate desire of people for fulfilment.

The other key inhibiting factor in our ability to achieve self-actualization is a failure of imagination. Being a musician, a poet or an artist requires imagination, creativity and innovation. Work in a corporate environment has traditionally discouraged these attributes. Creativity is seen as the realm of the marketing department and innovation is the responsibility of management. Encouraging people to express their creativity in whatever they do runs contrary to the idea of order and normality. This was something that worried Maslow. He asked 'why do people not create?' The reason is that neither management nor society, encourages it. Gordon MacKenzie, who worked at Hallmark Cards for 30 years as a creative director recounts a story that aptly demonstrates this. One of his activities was to go into schools and teach children about creativity – to foster the sort of 'disruption' he created in the institutional environment at Hallmark. When he arrived at a school, he would always tell the children that he was an artist and he would then observe the beautiful pictures the children had produced. He'd say that the pictures made him realize there must be lots of artists in the schoolroom. He'd ask 'how many artists are there in the room? Would you please raise your hands?'

The response was always the same:

First grade: En mass [sic] the children leapt from their chairs, arms waving wildly, eager hands trying to reach the ceiling. Every child was an artist.

Second grade: About half the kids raised their hands, shoulder high, no higher. The raised hands were still.

Third grade: At best, 10 kids out of 30 would raise a hand. Tentatively. Self-consciously.

And so on through the grades. The higher the grade, the fewer children raised their hands. By the time I reached sixth grade, no more than one or two did so and then only ever so-slightly – guardedly – their eyes glancing from side to side uneasily, betraying their fear of being identified by the group as a closet artist...The point now is:

Every school I visited was participating in the suppression of creative genius.

MacKenzie's point is that creativity is about challenging norms and finding new and original ways of doing things and that society suppresses this in the cause of sustainability and the protection of the status quo.[3] It's the same reason why the Ancient Greeks found Socrates' questioning of their ideas so uncomfortable and why he was sentenced to death for corrupting the minds of the young. And why Galileo's astronomical discoveries, which undermined the Biblical interpretation, led him to be tried by the Inquisition. Of course societies, like Imperial Spain – and business – which eschew creativity and suppress new ideas, tend to stagnate.

Despite these barriers to achieving self-actualization, Maslow's ideas about this need are powerful. When we move from the question 'Why do we work?' to 'Why do we choose to work where we do?' the fulfilment need becomes more dominant. If we have the choice, we will opt to work for organizations and environments that provide the opportunity to nurture our imagination and creativity; which extend our idea of what we are as individuals. The negation of this choice, causes us to feel dissatisfied with ourselves and, at the extreme, causes us psychological damage. At some point most of us have worked in what might be called dead-end jobs or roles where our opportunity to create new ideas was strictly limited. It makes us feel dispirited and trapped because we sense that we are not achieving our potential and that perhaps we could do so in another organization. This is what Heidegger calls inauthenticity: when we allow others to direct our lives rather than taking responsibility for what we are. In Maslow's view enlightened managers not only provide a safe, secure and social environment, but they also fulfil employees' 'metaneeds for truth and beauty and goodness and justice and perfection and law.'[4]

The implication of the need for self-actualization is that organisations need their Socrateses and their Galileos. For that to happen they have to create environments where freedom of expression is encouraged and creative genius stimulated. However, for this to be authentic, it has to be sincere. It cannot simply be a tactic to attract employees in a fiercely competitive labour market. It has to be part of a system of long-term organizational beliefs. The uncomfortable part for managers is that it requires trust in people – a willingness to accept that a well-focused workforce collectively has greater knowledge, intellectual capacity and better ideas than the board of directors.

Social

'I need we to be fully I.'[5]

One of the reasons people go to work is because of the opportunity to socialize. The question is 'why do people feel this need?' Although there are misanthropists, the evolution of humans suggests there is a causal link between brain size and socialization. From the early hominids to current humans there was a threefold increase in brain/body proportion. The evolution in brain size is associated with the requirements of participating in a complex, group-based social life. The study of personhood also gives us a clue as to our capacity to trust each other – and also to be disappointed by the betrayal of trust. One of the attributes of humans that separates us from other animals is our ability to recognize in others feelings that we ourselves have. We can identify with others because we can relate past and future events. If we see someone suffering the pain of bereavement we can recall our own similar experiences. When, for example, there is a flood or a famine and a charity asks us for money, we give because we can empathize with the individuals we see and we can imagine ourselves in a similar position. We can say, 'wouldn't it be terrible if we lost our home or didn't have anything to eat.' Only humans have this capacity – what is known as 'a representational theory of mind.' Chimpanzees can represent mental ideas based on actual objects, here and now, but it is only humans who can represent non-existent objects and link the past and future.[6] Armed with this power to identify our own experiences in others and with the need to work in groups, we can come to trust some of those around us. Yet, when that trust is broken we become embittered because it is a direct attack on our own identity.

Despite this need for socialization, society as a whole seems not to encourage it. In *Bowling Alone*[7] (the title comes from the phenomenon of people bowling alone while watching giant television screens; it is a direct contrast with the once very social aspect of bowling as epitomized in countless Hollywood films set in the 1950s and 1960s) – the social commentator, Robert Putnam argues that there is growing social isolation in the United States. People no longer vote in elections, nor seem much interested in the debates. The American magazine *Adbusters* (June/July 2000), notes that:

> news reports show that the American presidential wannabes are on pace to set records for campaign spending. By the time he came up for the Republican nomination George W. Bush had spent an unparalleled $50 million...Despite themes of greed, celebrity and democracy only three million viewers tuned in to the Republican presidential debate. With its themes of greed, celebrity and sex, 23 million opt for Fox TV's *Who Wants to Marry a Millionaire?*

Putnam goes on to argue that people socialize less with each other in the home and that there is a growing isolation within communities. These ideas are supported by Larry Keeley of the Doblin Group, which has conducted research into the nature of communities. Doblin's findings show that physical communities are being torn down and are not being replaced by Internet communities. Keeley says:

> hundreds of things showed us that people were not developing a relationship with others on the Internet. Instead they spend an enormous amount of time there and in so doing ignore their families and the immediate human beings that live around them. The former Librarian of Congress, Daniel Boorstin said that every advance in the history of communication has put us in touch with those who live far away at the expense of contact with those closest to us. Our research says, he's 100% right.

The causes of the failure to participate are various. The disappointment with politics is not confined to the United States where, in the early 1960s, three-quarters of those surveyed answered the question 'How many times can you trust the government in Washington to do what is right?' with 'most of the time.' Now less than four out of 10 trust the government to do what is right. Politicians in much of Europe and Japan are viewed with equal cynicism. For example, in Sweden the number of people disagreeing with the statement 'parties are only interested in people's votes not in their opinions' fell from 51 per cent in 1968 to 28 per cent in 1994.[8] Voting in the 1999 European elections fell overall to 49 per cent, from 57 per cent in 1994, with Britain the bottom of the pile with a voter turnout of 23.1 per cent. Partly, this disenchantment is because as we see more behind the scenes, we see the reality of political compromise and the feet of clay of even previously respected individuals. Partly, it is because politicians have brought the level of politics down through their seeming lack of ideology and the inauthentic language used to convey ideas.

Just as politics seems to be failing most people, traditional religion has lost the societal bonding role that it used to have in much of the Western world. As long ago as 1886 Emile Zola, declared that 'we have stopped believing in God, but not in our own immortality.' Research by the University of Michigan (1997) shows that the importance of religion has declined in the developed world. This is particularly notable in Northern Europe where on average less than 5 per cent of people attend church even once a week.

The impact of the denial of social involvement, or what Putnam would call social capital, tends to prove its need. Even though Americans have more wealth than ever before they also have the highest incidence of clinical depression and mental illness. Several research studies show that individuals who fail to build social networks are unhealthier, unhappier and more prone to committing crimes. In America, close to 25 million people now live alone and that figure is expected to rise by another five million over the next ten years.[9] Putnam calls for America to take note of this and to work towards building stronger communities through education and by encouraging organizations to take measures to alleviate some of the causes of bowling alone. Equally Doblin Group, through their long-term research into actual and virtual communities, argues that there needs to be a commitment to six general principles, if communities are to be sustainable:

- *effort*: obligation, participation, responsibility, collaboration, consequence;
- *purpose*: focus, influence, shared activity, progress, shared vision;
- *identity*: character, bounded, coherent, authentic, shared history, emergent;
- *organic*: decentralized, richness, co-constructued, interdependent, balanced;
- *adaptive*: flexible, scalable, responsive, resilient, feedback;
- *freedom*: rights, access, choice, empowering, fit.[10]

In spite of Putnam's persuasive arguments about the lack of community in society there is some evidence of countervailing forces. Even though people in the United States are perhaps less engaged than ever, the human need for community drives people to seek meaning elsewhere. For example in the United Kingdom, 48 per cent of the population has worked formally for a voluntary organization in the last year and 74 per cent either formally or informally. Internationally the number of non-governmental organizations (NGOs) has grown from 6,000 in 1990 to 26,000 in 1999 and membership of such high profile NGOs as the World Wide Fund for Nature (World Wildlife Fund in the United States) increased from 570,000 in 1985 to 5 million in 1999. As _The Economist_ says: 'Over the past decade, NGOs and their memberships have grown hugely...Democratisation and technological progress have revolutionised the way citizens can unite to express their disquiet.'[11]

As well as NGOs, some businesses have also recognized the virtue of creating environments that nurture social engagement. The motivations for this vary. For some it is the recognition of the benefits of contented and connected people. For others it's the corollary of people working longer hours[12] and the blurring of the boundaries of life and work. To this end companies provide everything from Bible classes to basketball clubs to employee service centres. The effect is to extend the relationships people have with their employers from purely work based into more complete social contracts. In one sense there is nothing new in this. Victorian paternalistic employers in Britain, such as the confectioner Cadbury and the retailer Whiteley's provided housing, education, welfare and sports facilities. However, the motivations now seem different. Much of what companies offer now seems to be as a substitute for the absence of socialization outside of work. The increasing specialization of work and the language associated with any specific area of expertise also makes it easier for many to enjoy the company of like-minded souls, rather than venture into environments where people's backgrounds might be very different. In many ways, socialization at work is a good thing. It is why, despite increased opportunities for virtual working, many still choose to spend at least part of their working week in an office environment. However, there are negatives. Business magazines, such as *Fast Company* and *Business 2.0* devote considerable attention to the problems of life/work balance such as overdependence and excessive expectations at work. At the extreme, if individuals devote their work time and their social time to the organization, what happens when the relationship ends? Whether the reason is termination of contract, acquisition by another company or retirement, the result is not only the cessation of financial certainty but the complete cessation of a social and economic context; the loss or reduction of all the attributes in Maslow's hierarchy. Many people see their life at work as an important determinant of meaning. It is what we spend most of our lives doing. It defines us as individuals. For some it specifies our social worth. It is a socializing environment. Yet if we are to lead some semblance of a balanced life, it should not be all consuming. We should have other networks and other interests.

Esteem

Maslow relates the concept of esteem to dignity. In the context in which he was writing, in the 1950s and 1960s, and given his stance against authoritarian management ideas, this terminology is not surprising. The need for dignity is universally understood even if it is not universally applied. Certainly the pervasive command and control approach that was prevalent often encouraged managers to ride roughshod over human sensibilities. Management was not in the business of nurturing the dignity or esteem of its employees; rather it was concerned with maximizing productivity. Much of the industrial strife that occurred in Europe in the 1960s and 1970s can be linked to the failure to recognize the need for esteem. British industrial relations were blighted for a generation because of the seeming intransigence of unions who were obsessed with demarcation of roles and the relativity of pay. The unions' desire to maintain the dignity of their members ran counter to the beliefs of management, which was desperate for greater flexibility and productivity from the workforce. With their entrenched views, each side denied the dignity of the other. Although Arthur Scargill, the leader of the National Union of Mineworkers (NUM) was vilified by the Thatcher government for his demands on pay, his continual refrain concerned his members' aspirations – in other words their needs as humans.

To recognize the importance of dignity to each of us as individuals just recall for a second an occasion when that dignity was denied: when you were called to account in front of others for a failure or when you were not given respect or when someone gloated when they bested you. Denial of our own dignity makes us angry. When it happens to others in our presence we can feel embarrassed and uncomfortable. In a work context, dignity is derived from the very fact of employment and from the nature of the employer/employee relationship. The fact of employment is important, because without it we have less opportunity to achieve the respect of others. The process of doing something valuable and of contributing something worthwhile motivates individuals and is the reason why purpose and value statements need to tap into this. The plaudits of peers, especially in areas such as software development, is a powerful motivating force. It is not uncommon for developers to use emotive, hyperbolic language in describing colleagues who have created innovative software. In particular, Linus Torvalds, who developed Linux and then made it freely available, is a revered hero in the information technology world.

The nature of the employment relationship is important, specifically to self-esteem. As Maslow pointed out, the esteem of others is important for wellbeing, but we also need to feel comfortable with ourselves. A relationship that suggests the individual is an important part of the organization, whose ideas and individuality is cherished is more likely to feel a sense of self-esteem, than someone whose daily activities are prescribed by the organizational hierarchy. Self-esteem is derived from the notion of being trusted by others and believing that we have the opportunity to express ourselves. It helps to receive plaudits, but ultimately we need to believe that we have made the right choices for ourselves.

Identification

Identification is concerned with people aligning their personal values with those of the organization. This must be an adaptive process, as the match can never be perfect. Indeed research by voluntary organization, VSO, among 1,000 adults, found that one in four people thought their values were different to their employers.[13] However, individuals find that some organizations better match their view of themselves and seem to provide better opportunities for self-actualization than others. Of course, choosing one organization in preference to another is judgmental for both sides. At the beginning, the organization and the individual will, through interviewing and testing, try to determine the likely match of values. Is this person right for the organization? Is the organization right for me? As well as the formal selection process, the individual will also be swayed by the image of the organization. For example, if one professes to be a person with liberal ideas, how would this equate with joining the armed services. It might be the case that armed services would welcome people with a liberal perspective, but if the organization's image is illiberal then the individual would probably not apply. One's perception of self can be extended by joining an organization where the match requires some adaptation, but to undertake a *volte face* would entail a fundamental questioning of personal values. At some times, this is a level of anxiety that people feel they want, but generally customs officers (with the exception of Henri Rousseau) do not become artists and musicians do not become investment bankers.

Although, Maslow was a believer in the importance of aligning the goals of the individual with those of the company, he was also moved to say, 'what is not worth doing is not worth doing well.' His view was that people will always prefer meaningful work to meaningless work, but that sometimes meaningful work is harder to find. If the work lacks meaning for the individual then it is not worth doing other than for safety and physiological needs. Of course, where one finds meaning will vary for the individual. A person who has a deep-seated belief in environmental causes may decide to join Greenpeace whereas a person who enjoys intellectual challenge may opt for an academic career. However, what of individuals who through a lack of academic qualifications or skills find themselves in repetitive or unchallenging jobs with little in the way of alternatives? If Maslow is right, there will still be an unmet need for identification. This will lead the individual to try to create that identification or they will seek it outside of a work environment.

Although most of us have come across or worked for organizations where there is little opportunity for fulfilment, some businesses have become adept at building identification. One excellent example of this is the Pike Place Fish Market in Seattle. Probably working on a fish stall from daybreak is not everyone's idea of fun but Pike Place has made a name for itself locally and internationally. It is even used as an example of how to deliver customer service in corporate training (in the UK, *Fish* was the top selling title for business training company Video Arts in 1999). The success of Pike Place is predicated on delivering exceptional service. The fish sellers do this by building a rapport with their customers. They come out into the hall area and talk to customers, they tell jokes and they hurl the fish from one side of the counter to the other. The sellers enjoy themselves and they share that sense of fun with passers by. Here are some other examples:

- Unipart is a car parts supplier. Many of the people who work for the organization do what might be called mundane jobs. However, the company has a belief in extending the skills of all its people. It has an in-house university, which has a central resource unit and locations on the shop floor, so that employees can study and participate in resolving work problems in innovative ways.
- Trailfinders is a travel agency with offices in the United Kingdom and overseas. It provides exceptional customer service in a cut-throat business. The workplace environment has a strong sales culture. Calls waiting to be dealt with, time on the phone and sales converted are all monitored and publicized. You might imagine this would lead to employees who are only

concerned with getting a sale as fast as they can, yet try the service and see the response. The company makes a difference by employing well-travelled people who love travel and everything to do with it. They tend to be well qualified and they're paid above the industry norms. The difference shows.[14]

- Virgin Atlantic has been written about with such frequency that it is almost a cliché. It stands out from the mediocrity of most of its competitors, because its employees so clearly believe in its fun, value for money and customer orientation. Virgin's purpose is about 'creating memorable moments for our customers'. Research by NOP on the Virgin brand shows that 83 per cent of people in the United Kingdom think that Virgin is friendly, 75 per cent say it is high quality, 68 per cent fun and 66 per cent innovative.

The implication of these examples is that any business has the potential to create meaning for its employees, to provide them with the opportunity for identification, if it stops to think about the core Maslowian needs that we all have. This is why there is often such a strong identification in the voluntary sector. Having worked with a number of charities, such as VSO, WWF and Unicef, what is observable is the passion individuals bring to organizational identification. The voluntary sector is relatively poorly paid but it scores well against the higher needs of esteem and self-actualization. This can make it difficult to focus employees' beliefs as they pursue their own interpretation of the organizational cause but it also has the potential to create extremely powerful brands.

The hierarchy of needs does not have the same strength for all of us. For a voluntary sector employee the need for identification is probably stronger than for others. This is perhaps why, in the United Kingdom, there has been significant growth in the number of people employed in the voluntary sector, from 336,000 in 1993 to 516,000 in 1997, a 53 per cent growth rate versus 5 per cent for the economy as a whole. Others will find that their needs change over time. For example, people sometimes discover the need to identify with a religion at times of personal crisis. Or the need to identify with an organization may diminish as someone fulfils a hitherto unmet desire to be an artist or a writer. Equally sometimes we might join an organization and feel the unity of personal and organizational goals, yet find some time later that everything has changed for the worse. Probably both sides have changed. This is a dynamic relationship with both sides seeking a fusion of identification.

Summary

Identification, then, is the fusion of self and organization, thereby helping to address one's 'existential needs for meaning, belonging, and even immortality.'[15]

Maslow's hierarchy of needs is an apt metaphor for why individuals need purpose and values at work. It demonstrates that individuals do not only seek the basic needs in life but also have what might be termed higher, spiritual needs. The American project Meaning at Work identifies the crucial factors in people's working lives as sense of purpose, oneness, ownership, fit and relationship building. For these higher needs to be met organizations have to change the way they think about individuals. It is not a case of cajoling or even commanding certain behaviours. If Maslow is right about the innateness of the needs then individuals are already seeking identification and esteem and self-actualization. The role of management is to clearly state what it believes in and to provide a framework in which individuals can flourish. The former will help to ensure that the organization and the potential employee are the right match for each other – that identification is not only possible but likely. The latter is about trusting the individual. These in themselves are not new ideas. Maslow started publishing in the 1930s, although it was only in the 1950s that he really started to concentrate on the individual in organizations, whereas Douglas McGregor's well-known, *The Human Side of Enterprise*, which juxtaposed authoritarian and collaborative managerial attitudes, appeared in 1960. What seems surprising is that their ideas about people's desires to learn and develop are still not met in large part by organizations. The benefits for organizations that do so are the subject of the next chapter.

Notes

1 Bartlett CA and Ghosal S (1994) Changing the role of top management: beyond strategy to purpose. *Harvard Business Review*, (November–December), p 81.
2 Maslow, Abraham (1998) *Maslow on Management*, John Wiley & Sons, Chichester, p 3.
3 MacKenzie, Gordon (1998) Orbiting the Giant Hairball, Viking Penguin, Harmondsworth, pp 19–20.
4 Maslow, Abraham (1998) *Maslow on Management*, John Wiley & Sons, Chichester, p 95.
5 Jung CG (1993) *The Basic Writings of CJ Jung*, ed V Staube de Laszlo, The Modern Library, New York.
6 Barresi, John (1999) On becoming a person, *Philosophical Psychology*, **12**, pp 79–98.
7 Putnam, Robert (2000) *Bowling Alone*, Simon and Schuster, New York.
8 Is there a crisis? *The Economist*, 17 July 1999.
9 USS Bureau of the Census.
10 See www.doblin.com for a bibliography and more details on communities.
11 Citizens groups: the non-governmental order, *The Economist*, 11 December 1999.
12 A Families and Work Institute survey found that the average working week for Americans increased from 43.6 hours in 1977 to 47.1 hours in 1997. However the tendency to work longer is not universal. In 1999 France formally adopted a 35-hour working week and the leisure-loving Scandinavians take six weeks of vacation a year compared to a miserly two to three weeks in the United States.
13 VSO (1999) *The Meaning of Work*, Research Report.
14 In an interview with *Management Today* (August 1999), Mike Gooley, founder of Trailfinders, says that his best decision was 'putting customers at the heart of the Trailfinders culture.' Talking about the company's employees he says: 'They work in a call-centre environment, but they aren't call-centre people. We give them respect and that flows through into the service they give to customers.'
15 Ashforth, Blake (1998) in Whetter, David and Godfrey, Paul (eds) *Identity in Organizations: Building theory through conversations*, Sage, London, p 268.

four

Why
organizations
need purpose
and values

'Many large organisations have the knack of taking in enthusiastic, committed and hopeful people and turning them, unwittingly and over time into hostile, cynical and hopeless people.'[1]

While the previous chapter explored the importance of purpose and values for individuals, this chapter will analyse why organizations need to engage employees with their overall purpose. This is vital if organizations are to use the full intellectual capital at their disposal. Often commentators write about organizations as abstract constructs and talk about value creation in terms of financial measures. What this ignores is that organizations are collections of people joined together in pursuit of a common cause and it is people who create value. In top-down, command-and-control organizations the abstract view often prevails and human resources professionals still bemoan the difficulties of persuading senior managers as to the importance of nurturing people. Largely this is because executives see the creation of intellectual capital as their preserve. They generate the ideas and create knowledge and then impart their wisdom to others to implement. Even when these organizations have employee suggestion schemes, quality circles and other forms of employee involvement, passing judgement on the input and refining ideas is seen as a top-level activity. This separation of the thinking from the doing survives because it is familiar and unthreatening. It relies on a militaristic model – which even the military now see as outdated – that stresses hierarchy and the power of status. Overall it does not require the wide dissemination of purpose and values, because management has control. There has been a long corporate love affair with this model. Companies have recruited strategy departments and planners, separated them out from the rest of the organization and then developed strategic plans based around any number of consultancy models. For those of an intellectual disposition this removal from organizational reality has been rather enjoyable. It is planning without the encumbrance of people. There are plenty of examples of the failure of this method, which perhaps proves Hegel's view that the lesson of history is that people and organizations never learn anything from the lessons of history.[2] One of the most insightful demonstrations of the limitations of planning – outside Soviet five-year plans – is the scheme that led to the First World War. It should be a salutary lesson for any would-be planner.

The plans for the German invasion of France, which heralded the First World War, had been in existence for some 20 years before its actual outbreak. Yet from the moment of their conception they were fundamentally flawed. As AJP Taylor says, 'Politically the plans for mobilisation were made in the void. They aimed at the best technical result without allowing for either the political conditions from which war might spring or the political consequences that might follow from any particular plan. There was little consultation between military planners and civilian statesmen…War had become a theoretical operation conducted for its own sake.'[3] The architect of the plan was Count von Schlieffen – a professor of strategy. He constructed a plan that would enable Germany to encircle Paris within six weeks. As a good planner should, he assessed the strength of the German armies relative to others; he created highly detailed plans and considered 'in his remorselessly academic way' the remotest contingencies. Yet the Germans never came close to Paris and were still fighting four years after the start of the war. Von Schlieffen made several fundamental oversights. He took no account of inexperienced troops, did not consider the impact of invading Belgian neutrality, overlooked the possibility of Great Britain entering the war and ignored the option that France would react with sufficient speed to halt the incursion. Despite this, others never questioned von Schlieffen's plan during its 20-year gestation because it became an article of faith within the German High Command.

The overwhelming reason for the failure of von Schlieffen's plan was that no attention was paid to the human element. The plan was an abstraction and didn't take into account Napoleon's dictum: it's the man in the plan that counts. Planning disasters are rarely intellectual power failures. In more recent times the group of people that advised Kennedy and then Johnson on Vietnam – Robert McNamara, Dean Rusk, McGeorge Bundy, Walt Rostow and Maxwell Taylor – were reputedly possessed of powerful intellects. In their fiercely academic way they analysed and advised. Yet when McNamara came to write his memoir and looked back at the record of meetings he was surprised at how little they knew of Vietnam and how often they failed to review key assumptions. As with Von Schlieffen, the view that a war in Vietnam could be won became the prevailing ethos. Military men and politicians who suggested otherwise received short shrift. To sustain this illusion the planners used casualty figures that were based on overly optimistic assumptions. This proved the war was being won, despite Ho Chi Minh's warning to the French in 1946 that 'you can kill ten of my men for every one I kill of yours, but even at these odds you will lose and I will win.'

A new model

Once we move away from abstract thinking we come to the realization that organizations build value through intellectual capital. It is the collective power of individuals in an organization that provides and sustains competitive advantage. As we saw in the previous chapter, it is becoming increasingly untenable to manage a business based solely on safety and physiological needs. Nor is it viable for management to maintain the hold they once had on organizational knowledge. The prevalence of information technology (IT) in organizations means that knowledge is everywhere. It cannot be managed in any true sense. Thus, business needs to engage the higher Maslowian needs. When people are engaged with the organization's purpose – and not just senior managers – then they generate new ways of working, share knowledge, stimulate innovation and help build brands. It enables organizations to adapt to changing circumstances, develop plans that are founded in organizational reality and deliver bottom-line value. Nowhere is this more in evidence than in the IT sector. How do some IT businesses generate such high turnovers and valuations when they have little in the way of physical assets? How is it that a company such as Qualcomm, the inventor of the mobile phone technology CDMA, can generate revenues of $4 billion a year by contracting others to make chipsets? The answer is through the intellectual capacity of its army of researchers and its patents and licensing. How did systems consultancy Scient create a successful business employing 1,800 professionals in two years? The answer lies in intellectual capital: the combination of Scient's clearly defined values, management capabilities, employee knowledge, methodologies and customer relationships. This position is reflected by the nature of the top 100 Fortune companies. The writer, Seth Godin points out that 20 years ago these top companies either dug something out of the ground or turned a natural resource into something. In the year 2000, more than half of the 100 made 'unseemly profits by trafficking in ideas.'[4] According to research by the Swedish insurance and financial services company Skandia, intellectual capital is the combination of human capital and structural capital. These two forms of capital can be defined as follows:

Human Capital: the combined knowledge, skills, innovativeness, and ability of the company's individual employees to meet the task at hand. It also includes the company's values, culture and philosophy. Human capital cannot be owned by the company.

Structural Capital: the hardware, software, databases, organizational structure, patents, trademarks, and everything else of organizational capability that supports those employees' productivity – in a word, everything left at the office when the employees go home. Structural capital also includes customer capital, the relationships developed with key customers. Unlike human capital, structural capital can be owned and thereby traded.[5]

Think of the ideas associated with building a brand through people and they can all be found in this definition:

- the collective knowledge and skill of employees;
- the organization's purpose and values;

- the relationships with customers;
- the commitment to innovation.

The organization's focus should be on encouraging all employees to maximize intellectual capital. This is not about managing but coaching. It is not about control but participation. It is not about being didactic but is about a dialogue. This is about living the brand. As Edvinsson and Malone state in their book, *Intellectual Capital*:

> Intellectual Capital will come to dominate the way we value our institutions because it alone captures the dynamics of organizational sustainability and value creation. It alone recognizes that a modern enterprise changes so fast that all it has left to depend on is the talents and dedication of its people and the quality of the tools they use.[6]

Thus, Intellectual Capital is at the heart of brand valuation and demonstrates the overwhelming need to focus on employing the most appropriate people and then nurturing their talents. This can only be achieved by creating a shared sense of purpose and values that generate real commitment. Thinking back to the previous chapter, the purpose is not likely to be about profit per se, but rather about enabling people to engage with an idea that is motivating and influential and one in which they play an active role.

Empowerment

Key to this model of organizations is the idea of empowerment. The word itself is overused in management thinking, but it is a vital process if the IQ quotient of an organization is to include all its members, rather than just its management. The problems with empowerment are:

- Managers often intellectually agree with the principle of giving power to individuals, but overlook the fact that this also means the diminution of their own power. For example, if a manager historically has had sole authority to set strategy for their business unit and then agrees to empower employees so that they too can have a say, this inevitably means a reduction in the power of the manager. The French philosopher Michel Foucault, who was an interested observer of the nature of power, recognized that relations of power dominate personal and organizational relations and that a gain in power by one group can only be at the expense of another. Thus managers need to recognize that empowerment contains an implicit reduction of individual influence for the benefit of the collective good. Empowerment does not diminish the importance of leadership. As long ago as the mid-1970s, Pehr Gyllenhammer, then President of Volvo, wrote: 'Leadership is crucial. Participation actually demands better leadership as well as more self-discipline from everyone involved.'[7]

The empowerment of employees can be paternalistic. Managers recognize the value of empowerment and then go through a process of consultation that is a parody of it: listening without really learning; talking without really trusting. The reality is that IT has already empowered individuals to a significant degree. If knowledge truly is power, the circulation of knowledge through intranets, extranets and direct interaction with people inside and outside the organization already enables many individuals to know as much as, if not more than, managers. In many organizations the company intranet is not only a noticeboard for information – it is a place where free and frank views about the organization are exchanged. It is neither desirable nor possible for management to control this process.

As speed becomes more important in business decision making, there is a feeling that it is quicker for managers to make a decision and for employees to implement it. This might have some plausibility in a smaller organization, but in a larger organization managers are too often divorced from operations to be the first to pick up on problems or opportunities. It is far more likely to be a customer-facing employee who notices a trend than a manager who has to rely on feedback from others or on market research. If employees are properly empowered they will react to their experience and then share it with others. At the operational level, an example of this is Xerox photocopier engineers. At the official level there is a handbook that instructs the engineers how to deal with problems. This explicit knowledge is useful to a certain extent, but in a study of what engineers actually do, it is the informal networking that is more powerful. Engineers learn about problems related to specific machines as they work and through talking to customers. This knowledge then becomes embedded through the casual day-to-day conversations that take place when the engineers meet for coffee or in the office. Sensibly, Xerox have recognized the reality of how the engineers work and have built a knowledge system, called Eureka that seeks to encourage the sharing of ideas: '...executives who want to identify and foster best practices must pay very close attention to the practices as they occur in reality rather than as they are represented in documentation or process designs. Otherwise, they will miss the tacit knowledge produced in improvisation, shared through story-telling, and embedded in the communities that form around those activities.'[8]

The argument against empowerment is that it has connotations of 1960s liberalism: a free-for-all where no one has responsibility and anarchy is just around the corner. However, empowerment in a corporate context can overcome this danger if people are engaged by the organization's values. This provides the range within which people can be free. Rather than seeing liberalism as a dangerous force, it should be seen as a means of questioning and stimulating change. This is far more likely to be achieved by committed individuals with little investment in the status quo than stock-optioned top management who, as Gary Hamel has pointed out, 'can be expected to prefer low-risk strategies for pumping up the share price.'

The benefits of empowering employees

Frequently companies start on the process of encouraging employees to live the brand and then as change becomes uncomfortable they look for evidence of the likely benefits. Over the last 20 years several studies have provided substantive evidence. Probably most notable was a study led by David Lewin, which covered 495 organizations and used statistical techniques to identify the causal relationships between human resource practices and bottom line performance. The study concluded that:

- Companies that share profits and gains with employees have significantly better financial performance than those that do not.
- Companies that share information broadly and have broad programmes of employee involvement (the researchers define involvement as areas of intellectual participation) perform significantly better than companies that are run autocratically.
- Flexible work design (flexible hours, rotation and job enlargement) is significantly related to financial success.
- Training and development have a positive effect on business financial performance.
- Two-thirds of the bottom-line impact was due to the combined effect of group economic participation, intellectual participation, flexible job design, and training and development.[9]

Supporting Lewin's views are the range of studies cited by Jeffrey Pfeffer in his book, *The Human Equation*. Pfeffer provides evidence from analyses of the automobile industry, steel, apparel, semiconductors, oil refining and services. Each of the examples is powerfully argued but, as an indicator, the example below relates to steel minimills. In this analysis 30 minimills in the United States were studied. The mills were grouped according to how they were managed. One group was categorized as 'control led'. Here the focus was on reducing labour costs, enforcing compliance with procedures and rewarding people based on measurable output. The other management style was categorized as 'commitment'. Here we see higher Maslowian attitudes prevailing where there is a considered attempt to align individual and corporate goals and a focus on developing committed employees who can be trusted to carry out tasks. From Table 4.1 it can be seen that commitment systems pay better, use more skilled staff, encourage people to work in teams, are more decentralized and provide more training.

These differences in themselves make interesting reading but it is the fact that a commitment strategy significantly impacts on performance that emphasizes the real value. Minimills that use commitment-oriented management required 34 per cent fewer labour hours to produce a ton of steel and showed a 65 per cent better scrap rate.[10]

Table 4.1: Control and commitment

Management practice	Control	Commitment	Percentage difference
Wages	$18.07	$21.52	19.1
Skill (maintenance and craft workers as percentage of all employees)	14.0	19.0	35.7
Percentage in teams or small problem solving groups	36.6	52.4	43.1
Decentralisation (1 = very little to 6 = very much)	2.42	3.04	25.6
General training	1.92	3.35	74.5

Source: Arthur, Jeffrey B (1995) Effects of human resource systems on manufacturing performance and turnover, *Academy of Management Journal*, 37, p 676

Finally a study conducted in the United Kingdom into empowerment by the manufacturing consultancy practice, Bourton Group, and published in 1998 also demonstrates the value to business of empowerment. Bourton collected information on 100 UK manufacturing companies including the degree to which they employed empowerment principles. The companies were examined over a four-year period against:

- sales revenue growth;
- return on sales improvement;
- return on capital employed improvement;
- increase in profit per employee.

For each measure, Bourton took the companies in the upper quartile for performance and found significant gains but most notable was that 'there were significantly more empowered businesses within this upper quartile compared to businesses with a more traditional approach.' The analysis also demonstrated that the more highly empowered firms 'are more than twice as likely to show improvements on critical financial indicators than the below average firms over a four year period.' Figure 4.1 compares the upper quartile performance of empowered versus traditional companies and supports Bourton's view that 'empowering your employees can make good profitable sense.'[11]

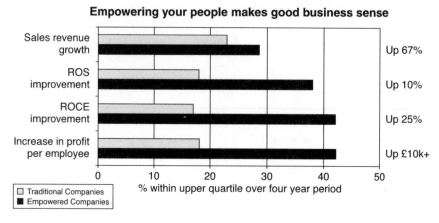

Figure 4.1 The power of empowerment

These studies by Lewin and Bourton, and others, demonstrate that empowered companies tend to be strong performers. They prove that Maslow and McGregor were right to argue that organizations should adopt an 'employee-centric' approach to management. The question is whether this emphasis is viable for all types of organizations? No doubt traditionally run companies would claim that empowerment is not always effective and that the costs of empowerment can outweigh the benefits. This argument is most often put forward either by companies that have charismatic managers who want to lead their organizations to victory or by companies with well-defined systems that believe that it is the controlled continuity of performance that achieves results.

As a counterpoint to the former view, look at the innovation that is generated by Sir Richard Branson's Virgin Group. This organization is sometimes criticized for the breadth of businesses it operates in, which include everything from trains to planes, financial services to cosmetics, wine to soft drinks. However, there is a unity to the business in that all the manifestations of the Virgin brand have a youthful, customer focused, kick-ass quality. Is this business more than the charismatic Branson? Branson certainly sets the tone and has a very high public profile, but the surprise is that much of the innovation within Virgin is a direct result of empowerment. The company has a motto, which is 'screw it, let's do it.' As a consequence there is a vibrant internal market for ideas within Virgin.

Rather than employees huddling together secretly to plot new businesses, draw up plans and seek external funding, they know that if they have a good business idea they will always get a hearing internally. Take the example of Ailsa Petchey, a flight attendant on Virgin Atlantic. She was helping a friend to organize a wedding: booking the venue, finding the dressmakers, ordering the flowers and drawing up the guest list. Anyone who has been through the process will know this is a particularly stressful exercise. Not only do you have a wide array of different people to appease but you have to rely on an army of suppliers, any one of whom can let you down at the last minute. Petchey reasoned that it would be much easier if there was a one-stop shop where you could organize and buy everything. She took the idea to Branson and the result is Virgin Brides – a chain of shops that cater for everything the would-be bride needs. Petchey is its European head of marketing. As Gary Hamel, writing in *Fortune* says, 'Could this happen in your company? Could a twentysomething first-line employee buttonhole the chairman and get permission to start a new business?'[12] In the long term, Virgin Brides might or might not be a success but the important aspects are that Virgin was prepared to take the risk and to give its name to it. It is only willing to do this if the business concept is consonant with the idea of the Virgin brand. The compromise solution, which companies sometimes adopt, is to fund a business but to use a different brand name. However, this immediately reduces the chances of success. Not only does the new venture have to work harder to establish itself without the support of the umbrella brand – it also indicates a lack of faith in the concept. True empowerment requires courage not compromise.

The other argument against empowerment is applied by organizations that have well-developed operating systems. The rationale is there is no need for empowerment because the way of doing things is already proscribed. The benefit of a strong systems-led approach is the potential continuity of experience: the McDonald's ethos, where the consumer experience is largely consistent everywhere you encounter the brand. However, empowerment does not necessarily supplant a systematic approach. Even in empowered organizations there are clear methodologies. Empowerment allows employees to use their judgement to adjust the system to meet the needs of consumers. There is nothing more frustrating as a consumer than to be told you cannot do or have something because of adherence by employees to a rule book and perhaps nothing more welcome than an employee who can deliver exceptional service because he or she can step outside the framework. For example, at American retailer, Nordstrom, the company spends little on training its sales staff and provides no guidance to its highly empowered employees other than a postcard that announces that there is only one rule at Nordstrom: to use good judgement in all situations. This means that if you visit a Nordstrom store and the product you want is unavailable, the sales staff will not simply dismiss you – they will check stock availability, ring around other stores and even get the item for you if the next branch is nearby. This is what Jan Carlzon, one-time head of SAS, called 'moments of truth'. He recognized that it is the details of inter-action that determine customer perceptions of an organization.[13] The sum of the moments defines whether we feel positive or negative about an experience. When people go out of their way to deliver exceptional service it makes us feel special as individuals. This cannot be achieved by telling employees to do things as it is impos-sible to legislate for every eventuality. It can only happen when people believe in the organization's brand. In reality, a rulebook is no longer viable outside of bureaucracies. Increasingly, consumers expect high levels of service and customization by right. If you don't deliver what people want they will go elsewhere, including the Web, which offers the option of a vastly increased choice. The shift in power from the company to the consumer is fact. Companies like Dell were created around the idea of build to order. When people have contact with a company either by the Web or face to face they want a dialogue. The Web sites that work least well are those that deny consumer pre-eminence. Didactic sites often lead you into frus-tration because they deny choice and lead you down dead end paths.

Just as consumers have dominance, so do clients in business to business relationships. Whereas sales-led organizations focus on generating systems that enable operational efficiency, research con-sistently shows that clients want adaptability. Their circumstances are always unique and they want computers, software, people, raw materials and finance that meet their needs – not a lowest common denominator, one-size-fits-all, service. This requires employees who can listen to customers and have the freedom to create appropriate solutions. This surprisingly simple premise seems however to be ignored by a large number of companies, which, while ironically claiming flexibility and adaptability in their corporate principles, fail to deliver.

The value of ideology

From its launch in San Francisco in 1998, the systems innovation company, Scient, defined a clear ideology. Its founders wanted to create a dynamic organization that could grow rapidly, was exciting to work in and challenged its employees. The organization's purpose and values therefore contain different focal points. Success within Scient is not measured simply by generating a healthy profit or being a good consultant. It is a combination of the individual's contribution to clients, to the company and to colleagues. Holding these elements together is the vision statement and the values. The vision is: 'to be the high value provider of innovative electronic business services that create market leadership, breakthrough positions and shareholder value for our clients.' The values, detailed below were also formulated at the start and, although the culture has changed as the company has grown and experienced the tribulations of a volatile market, the values have remained constant. They are the guiding light for behaviour. The difficulty is that, while start-up individuals can agree among themselves what they are trying to be and what they believe in, when you're suddenly employing 500 people and then 1,000, you have to ensure the ideology is effectively embedded. To achieve this, Scient have a number of ideological proselytizers, but they also have the processes in place to ensure employees live and breathe the ideology.

Scient core values

Innovation:

- intellect, imagination and creativity our credo;
- high-impact ideas and achievements our stock in trade;
- value creation our way of life.

Excellence

- client satisfaction paramount;
- integrity in all we do;
- quality without compromise;
- outstanding execution always;
- accountable for our actions.

Urgency

- commitment to deliver, all the time;
- strong work ethic the norm;
- focus on winning for everyone;
- our results speak for themselves.

Community

- teamwork by all;
- open and honest dealings;
- recognition and achievements;
- leadership at every level;
- caring for others;
- trust.

Spirit

- respect for the individual;
- everyone an owner, empowered to succeed;
- non-political meritocracy;
- fun evironment;
- courage to be different.

Growth

- personal and professional opportunity;
- teaching organization: learning and knowledge, sharing a way of life;
- mentoring and guidance for all;
- open minded to new ideas.

The vision and values and a description of the organizational culture feature on the company's Web site, so that any would-be employee, partner or client has a clear expectation of the Scient brand. The values then form a part of an employee interview process. The goal at this stage is to determine whether there is a good fit between the individual and the organization's values. Once employed, the new Scient employee is sent off on a five-day programme called SPARK (the acronym stands for Scient: Performance; Achievement; Results; Knowledge). The idea of SPARK is to immerse people in the culture and the meaning behind the values: what does Spirit mean for the way you work day to day? How do you contribute to the idea of Community? If people are going to be empowered, which they have to be in such a fast-moving environment, they need to know what the values truly mean. Employees know they work in a meritocracy and their ideas and decisions have real impact. The corollary of this is that while people are empowered, they are not abandoned. There is a supportive structure and consultants are always encouraged to seek advice and help if they encounter a problem or get into trouble.

Once an employee starts working for Scient, the indoctrination continues. Employees are bombarded by slogans designed to reinforce the values – they're on T-shirts, in the company literature and printed on the walls.

- 'It takes courage to do legendary work.'
- 'Here today, gone later today.'
- ' If it's worth doing, it's worth doing wrong, fast.'
- ' If you haven't changed your mind recently, how do you know you have one?'

Meetings often turn to the values to decide issues and the values are talked about all the time. If this smacks of cultism it is probably a notion with which Scient would feel quite comfortable. Chris Lochhead, Chief Marketing Officer, sounds like an evangelist:

> We won't compromise ourselves. If internally our people felt we were selling out our values and our culture and our raison d'être they would leave...The only reason we come to work here everyday is we think this is the best place in the world to be.

As with Patagonia, one of the keys to Scient's business model is the blurring of the boundaries between internal and external. This is part of the courage to be open and to say the same things to employees and to clients. The sense of ambition that is inculcated into staff also extends into the client base. Lochhead says, 'to be a client, you'd better want to build the market dominating eBusiness in your market.'

The lesson of Scient is that a core ideology brings the brand to life in people's day-to-day lives and enhances performance. If one took away the clarity that underpins the ideology the company would not have been able to grow at such speed. It is the combination of empowerment of individuals and the strength of the purpose that allows for such well-focused devolution to business teams and locations across the world. Of course, Scient is a fast company so the question can be posed as to whether a core ideology is important to long-established businesses? Do they, too, benefit from clarity or does longevity nullify the impact of an ideological position? Rapid growth may be one driver of the need for cohesion, but so is the desire for sustainability. Organizations that grow and develop over time need glue to hold them together. In the beginning there is often the ideals of a founder directing events, but any organization will also encounter shifting fortunes, crises, changes in personnel, new business innovations and a changing business environment. Just look at the example of the Finnish company Nokia and the changes it has encountered since its founding in 1865. Nokia takes its name from a lumber mill on the banks of the Nokia River in Finland. Over 130 years Nokia moved from trees and into diapers, rubber products, power transmission and telephone cables. Finally it moved into electronics and telecommunications, but it was not clear that areas such as mobile phones had a great potential in the company. Following the break up of the USSR and the consequent free fall of the Finnish economy, Nokia debated selling its mobile division, except that no one seemed interested in buying it. Yet by 1999, Nokia had a 27 per cent market share of the mobile phone market, easily outpacing Motorola and Ericsson and close to 70 per cent of the global profits generated by the industry. By market capitalization it was also the second largest company in Europe and in terms of its brand valuation, it is rated fifth in the world. The ideology that holds the company together is built around the concept of the Nokia Way (see Figure 4.2).

Part of the process of sustaining the Nokia Way is an annual programme of analysis and presentations, using the values as a starting point, in which employees all over the world participate. This leads to the ongoing development of the strategic vision, so that the company is always at the forefront of developments, without losing the essence of the brand.

In their influential book, *Built to Last*,[14] James Collins and Jerry Porras identified 18 visionary and long-established companies (pre-1950) and compared them with 18 merely good organizations. Their conclusion was:

> Throughout the history of most of the visionary companies we saw a core ideology that transcended purely economic considerations. And – this is the key point – they have had core ideology to a greater degree than the comparison companies in our study.

The Nokia Way

Nokia is proud of its historical and current commitment to being a company based upon principles and values. A few fundamental and inter-related values and principles unite the company across its locations and form the basis of Nokia's distinctive culture as well as its business success. These values and principles will continue to provide the foundation for our long-term success also in the future.

Nokia Values

The Nokia Values are a statement of how Nokia should operate and a cornerstone of the company's corporate culture. They are the standards of behavior expected of all Nokia employees. The values form a common bond and language as well as a shared philosophy for working together.

Nokia's values are Customer Satisfaction, Respect for the Individual, Achievement and Continuous Learning. Customer satisfaction is the basis of all Nokia's operations. Respect for the Individual means that Nokia believes in the individual, whether she or he is an employee, a business partner or a customer. It also means open and candid communication, fairness, mutual trust and acceptance of diversity. Achieving results requires that every Nokia employee is working according to a strategy and well-defined goals. Everyone in the company must know the goals of the company as well as those set for him or her. To be a leader in the telecommunications industry takes innovation, courage and a constant willingness to learn. Continuous learning means that everyone is entitled to look for ways to improve their performance.

Nokia wants to create an environment where employees, customers and suppliers and other cooperation partners feel the empowerment to develop and improve their relations through a common exchange and development of ideas.

Figure 4.2 The Nokia Way

Collins and Porras believed that it was the combination of a deeply rooted purpose, such as Hewlett Packard's 'to make technical contributions for the advancement and welfare of humanity', or 3M's 'to solve unsolved problems innovatively', and the commitment to progress that enabled the visionary companies to stay ahead. The comparison companies often had ideologies as well, but as the quote above suggests it is the sincerity of the ideology and the commitment to it that differentiates the visionary company. This quasi-religious environment, ensures that the purpose and values are deeply ingrained. They're all-pervasive and they dominate thinking. Ideology defines the organization's direction and provides a credo with which employees can engage. The danger with ideologies is that they become too tightly defining and prevent organizations from seeing opportunities. Xerox was a prime example of this. It was exceptionally good at invention and poor at innovation. Its Palo Alto Research Center spawned inventive concepts but the company failed to capitalize on them. Ideas such as double click technology have been commercialized elsewhere by Apple and Microsoft. Why did Xerox miss out? Largely because of its horizons – the company saw itself as a copier company and therefore ignored inventions that would have taken it into printers and computers. It is a variation on the Von Schlieffen syndrome that shuts out alternatives and opportunities.

The balancing act is to articulate an ideology that has sufficient latitude to enable an organization to cope with change but has sufficient rigour to enable focus. Thus, perhaps, Xerox should think itself as an organization that enables the sharing of knowledge. This would encourage its inventors to develop ideas that work in the electronic and print medium and to think of applications that take in the Web. Rather than losing those inventions, the company could then become an innovator, marketing the ideas under its brand name. Equally, the oil companies have increasingly realized that their long-term future lies 'beyond petroleum', which is why BP Amoco (formerly BP stood for British Petroleum) has redefined the meaning behind its acronym to take in this idea. Now BP sees itself as an energy solutions company and is the world's leading producer of solar power. Similarly Shell has established a division called International Renewables, which takes in wind, solar and biomass power. BP and Shell are not waiting to see whether their traditional source of business runs out – they are working with a broader interpretation of their ideologies. If either company had seen itself as purely an oil company it would be excluding new opportunities. The point about Hewlett Packard, 3M, BP and Shell, is that their sense of self is not constrained by the specifics of what they do. Rather it is based around an ambition that is independent of computers, adhesives and oil. These companies envision their sense of the future and their role within it and they then set up the mechanisms to take them towards their goal. In a sense, these goals are infinite: 3M is unlikely to run out of opportunities to 'solve unsolved problems, innovatively.' All that is required is the purpose and the quality of people to achieve it.

Attracting and retaining employees

The key battleground for many companies is people. Take the IT sector. In this industry demand outstrips supply. This situation will not apply forever but while digital communications continue to develop the main constraint on growth is attracting and then retaining the right quality of people. The main advantage companies in this industry enjoy is their external profile built around their core values. For example, when the digital business consultancy Icon Medialab was founded in 1996 in Stockholm it defined a set of ideas to steer the company: fun, fame, fortune, future. In other words, it would seek to take on projects that would be fun for its employees to work on. Projects that would be challenging and that would create a reputation for its clients. Projects that would generate high revenues to enable the company to grow rapidly and that would enrich the people that worked for it. And projects that would define the future so that people would have a sense of influencing the industry in which they worked. The four 'Fs' are designed to affect the way people behave internally and the way they interact with clients. In Sweden, where the company employs some 500 people (September 2000), it is front-page news. Interviews with employees appear on national television, in the popular press and in the business news. Even people on the street know of Icon Medialab. Icon is well known because it is opinionated. One of its founders, Johan Staël von Holstein, is particularly infamous, not least because he is highly critical of the Swedish government and its Prime Minister. However, more than this, it is the idiosyncratic values that distinguish the company from its competitors. It wears its values on its sleeve. The impact of this is that the company can attract people who have a similar value set. It is unlikely to encourage people who want a highly structured environment or believe in the Scandinavian tradition of Janteloven – the idea, expounded in a novel by the Danish-born writer Aksel Sandemose, that people should not see themselves as better than others.[15] It does appeal strongly to individuals who are ambitious and motivated and like the idea of having the freedom to experiment. If the company was bland it might have a wider appeal, but it would not generate the same profile or indeed commitment from its people.

These new businesses enjoy the interest that comes with being young and high profile. However, other long-established companies, if they create a clear image of the organization, can also enjoy an aura that attracts individuals. In Silicon Valley terms, Adobe Systems is an old company. It started in 1982 developing software solutions for print publishing. Now it is an international company with 3,000 employees around the world and with revenues of $1 billion plus (April 2000). The driver for Adobe to clearly articulate and communicate its vision and values internally and externally was the need to attract and retain people. Melissa Dyrdahl, Senior Vice President of Corporate Marketing, says:

> For a high tech company we're pretty old. We're in an industry that's incredibly dynamic and is changing at an incredibly fast rate…we're playing in a market where there are lots of cooler, edgier companies.

In this competitive environment, Adobe had to work on enhancing its external image while remaining true to its values. The output was a new approach to communications and a greater commitment to external marketing spend, alongside an internal communications programme that conveyed the idea of the brand to employees. Adobe was conscious that it couldn't stretch its brand too far, but that it needed to overlay a hipper image over its traditional virtues such as being customer focused and innovative. Remaining true to

Adobe's virtues was important, because the image is not just a result of advertising, but rather all the interactions with the organization – particularly word of mouth. Dyrdahl says:

> A lot of the reasons people join a company and stay with it are to do with intangibles – the culture and the brand. Do I want to say I work at Adobe? Is that cool? When I tell people I work at Adobe, people say wow!

The Adobe brand seems to comprise the stability and structure of a well-established organization together with a creative and challenging culture that is a result of the principles of the founders and the nature of the products. It is why Adobe is ranked in the top 100 companies to work for in America by *Fortune* magazine and one of the top 10 companies by *Interactive Week* magazine.

While having a strong external image is important for recruitment it is also an important element in retention of people. The way people think an organization is seen by others is important for their self-esteem. It's always better if people say 'wow!' when you explain whom you work for, than if they look sympathetic and say 'who?' Our awareness of how we seem in the consciousness of others colours and transforms our lives. One of the most interesting studies on the impact of external image on internal identity was that of the New York Port Authority.[16] The Port Authority had to confront the problem of homelessness within New York because of the use of the Authority locations by the homeless. The reactions of the Authority were driven by criticism of their handling of the issue and the way in which individuals who worked for the Authority saw their sense of self diminished as a result of their association with the organization. The identity and image of the Authority defined their responses and led to an evolving interpretation of the problem:

- Phase 1 – homelessness is a police-security issue.
- Phase 2 – homelessness is a corporate issue but the Port Authority is not in the social service business.
- Phase 3 – homelessness is a business problem and needs moral solutions.
- Phase 4 – homelessness is an issue of regional image and no one else will solve it

■ Phase 5 – homelessness is linked to other regional problems; homelessness in transportation facilities are unique and need advocates.

As the case writers Jane Dutton and Janet Dukerich say:

An organization's image matters greatly to its members because it represents members' best guesses at what characteristics others are likely to ascribe to them because of their organizational affiliation.[17]

When the Port Authority employees saw their sense of their own professionalism and public service ethic criticized in the media they became very angry. This indicates that the willingness of employees to be identified with an organization will vary depending on how they believe the organization is seen by others and suggests the importance of linking together internal and external communications. Employees are more inclined to stay with an organization if it promotes rather than undermines their self-esteem. Generally this is beneficial to the brand. The longer people stay with an organization, the better they come to understand the culture and the systems and the better able they are to build a bond of trust with customers and partners. Thus retention strengthens the brand and enhances intellectual capital. Of course, retention figures will vary depending on location and industry type. Urban areas where people have plenty of opportunities to choose from and sales environments tend to encourage higher staff turnover rates, but good companies can often buck the trends. For example, Cisco Systems has a voluntary turnover rate of just 5 per cent per year, the much-lauded Southwest Airlines 7 per cent and energy company Enron 4 per cent.

However, voluntary turnover should not be an absolute guide to the power of the brand. Sometimes organizations seem to have relatively high staff turnover rates, yet are good at the long-term retention of a core of people. This might indicate that selection and early training procedures are at fault. Too many brand rejecters, suggests the alignment between individual and corporate values and aspirations is poor. Even the US retailer, Nordstrom, which is consistently praised for the quality of its service and as a place for work, has a 43 per cent staff turnover rate. Yet 3,000 of Nordstrom's staff (just fewer than 10 per cent of the total) have been in place for 10 years and 34 out of the 36 corporate officers came from the stock room or the sales floor. It shows that Nordstrom's distinctive brand, with its obsessive belief in empowerment, is alienating for many but deeply appealing for some. The long servers are the real brand champions – the storytellers who spread the idea of the brand to colleagues and customers.[18] Although the majority of employees are not true brand champions, the goal should be to influence and convert the waverers in the outer rings.

Champions are vital in countering the transient employees and also the non-standard workers (part-time, independent contractors, temporary and self-employed) who represent 24.8 per cent of the jobs

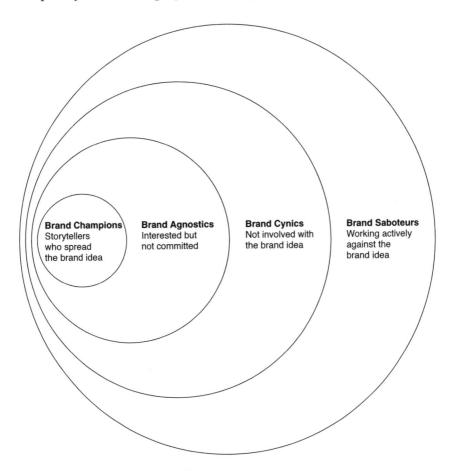

Figure 4.3 The power of brand champions

in the United States. The degree of commitment of the latter group tends to vary considerably and depends on their motivation for what is known as contingent work. When individuals see contingent work as a route to full-time employment that can be just as committed as full-time workers, but many individuals choose it because it reduces their commitment and they can then spend more time with family or pursuing other interests. Sometimes, contingent work is all that the organization offers an individual. For the organization there are benefits: first, contingent workers are often paid less and do not often receive the same benefit packages as full-time workers (however, legislation may change this); second, it provides flexibility so that companies can more easily increase and reduce their workforces as market conditions dictate and avoid the negative publicity of layoffs.

The suggestion here is not that organizations should abandon flexible work practices but that they should commit to trying to engage all their employees, whatever the nature of their employment contract, with the organization's purpose. This will probably always be easier to achieve with full-time employees who have consciously chosen the organization, but it is a too-often repeated claim by contractors and temporaries that they feel like second-class citizens, excluded from the mainstream of the organization. An inclusive approach, which stresses the importance of the organizational values is preferable because it encourages individuals to be brand communicators. It is worthwhile to remember contingent workers are probably more powerful word-of-mouth advocates or saboteurs than full-time staff, by virtue of the number of organizations with which they come into contact.

Certainty and Uncertainty

Brands are founded on the principle of certainty – the idea that the product you buy this week, will be the same as the previous week. This idea also carries through to service brands, although, this is often hard to achieve. It is simply not possible to order people to behave in an entirely predictable way. This situation is exacerbated by the increasing scale and internationalization of businesses. As organizations grow they become increasingly fragmented.

Departments start to acquire their own identities and countries bring their own cultural prejudices to a business. Consequently the experience of visiting Disneyland in France is not the same as visiting Disney in the United States. While harmonization is, to a degree, possible it is not always desirable – service expectations are not consistent and the tone of delivery of a message that might be appropriate in America may make a European cringe. More than this, we do not always want consistency. While we might be shocked if every time we bought a tin of beans it tasted different, in other markets we do want unpredictability. Predictability can be boring. If we regularly go to an art gallery such as Tate Modern in London or the Museum of Metropolitan Art in New York, we would soon be bored if there was no variety. Equally, if we go to buy books at Amazon and there is absolute consistency in the presentation and offer, we are not tempted to venture into areas that we might otherwise ignore. Eventually we brand switch to Barnes & Noble in search of something different; a new experience. As individuals we want the reassurance of the familiar *and* the adventure of the unknown. One of the recent media trends is the development of personal portals, such as MyCNN. The value of these portals is that they help us when we are overwhelmed by the volume of information we have to cope with. The proliferation of print titles, the impact of digital television and the scale of the Web mean that we have more information than ever before, but to make sense of it all we need filtering mechanisms. The personalized portal means we can select those areas are that are of most interest to us. Yet, this filtering, while valuable, denies us the benefit of serendipity. Part of the fulfilment of reading a print-based title is that although we might focus on the areas in which we are most interested, such as sport and business, we can become engaged by the latest piece of gossip from Hollywood, a sex scandal or an obituary. The element of surprise, therefore, is a key component of the reading experience. The writer Marcel Proust was a particular devotee of newspapers and would read them assiduously, not so much because he wished to be well informed but because they surprised and spurred his imagination. Proust enjoyed the idea of taking the banal and the commonplace and creating imaginary worlds, even to the extent that he was a reader of railway timetables.

Imaginative individuals in organizations create brands that provide new experiences, by innovating within the guidelines defined by purpose and values. Apple Computer's core theme of 'insanely great computers' and their empowering ideal of changing the way people work, learn, think and communicate was the ideal context for Jonathan Ive to develop the Apple iMac – a computer which uses aesthetics to differentiate itself. When you have an organization that encourages you to think the unthinkable and to question assumptions, you can change the fundamentals of an industry. The iMac sold 400,000 units in its first month and spawned a change in the way computers are designed. For the consumer, the iMac was undoubtedly a new style of computer, but from the launch of the Macintosh in 1984 Apple has always innovated. Surprise is an essential part of the brand. Equally, Nike is always innovating. Like Apple, it incorporates surprise into the brand, but it too innovates based on a core premise. Nike has a belief in sporting excellence and iconoclasm. This is unified within the idea of 'irreverence justified'. This was originally a headline written for an advertisement but it has come to represent the spirit of Nike: the notion that Nike's irreverent, challenging approach is justified by its focus on quality. This is how Nelson Farris, Nike's chief storyteller describes the idea:

> Irreverence came from looking at the sports establishment and saying it hasn't changed. If we're going to make inroads we have to challenge. Everything was based on supporting the cause of the athlete. If the athletes were going to fight the system to make it better we'd support that. We supported changes in running and basketball. Irreverence was there from day one, because we had nothing, so we had to fight our way. We reinvented the entire process of thinking about and delivering sporting goods. We looked at the business differently. So the irreverence was we didn't know what we were doing; we thought it could all be done better; we fought for the rights and causes of athletes and we supported it in our ads. We used to run ads, attacking the IOC, because they wouldn't let women run in longer distance races. They were so out of touch. We were not afraid to prod the system.

Apple and Nike are powerful brands because they provide both certainty and uncertainty. The individuals within these companies that create new ideas are able to use the focus of the organizational ideology as a starting point. This sets the context for innovation. There is an appealing symmetry in the challenging and people focused design of the first Macintosh and the iMac. Similarly, there is an appealing continuity between the way Bill Bowerman, one of the founders of Nike, created the company's first signature shoe – the waffle-soled running trainer – in the early 1970s and the designer who created the Goatek shoe in 1999. The waffle shoe acquired its name, because when Bowerman was trying to create a shoe with better traction, he found himself sitting at home at the kitchen table in front of a waffle iron. Looking at the pattern of the iron he saw the shape of square running spikes. Fast forward 30 years and a Nike designer was trying to think through the challenge of creating a running shoe that would provide excellent traction for people with flat feet. The inspiration was watching mountain goats and wondering how they managed to maintain their grip on such difficult terrain. The Goatek replicates the shape of a goat's foot and uses sticky rubber, so that it doesn't slip. The Goatek is an irreverent idea, but it is clearly within the cultural context of innovation within Nike.

The barriers

The weight of evidence detailed in the previous sections would make one think that building a clear purpose and values and then sustaining them through appropriate mechanisms would be a requirement for all businesses. Yet there are powerful barriers that prevent the effective adoption of this ideal. Research in 1999 by Opinion Research Corporation International (ORC) among 100 senior corporate communicators from major organizations shows that often brand mission, vision and values are rooted among senior managers, but do not permeate the rest of the organization. The scores are lowest for Europe, where only 36 per cent of interviewees thought the brand mission, vision and values were disseminated and believed in by employees.

Qualitative input to the research suggests that the failure to engage employees in many cases is 'because senior management have been instrumental in creating the messages but less effective

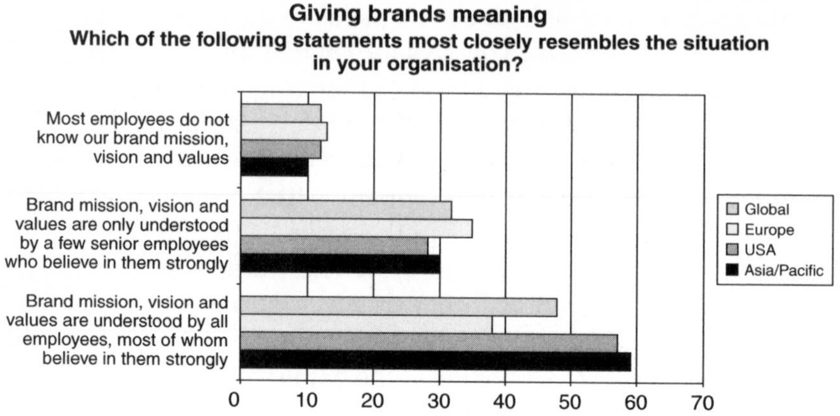

Giving brands meaning
Which of the following statements most closely resembles the situation in your organisation?

Source: ORC International, 1999

Figure 4.4 Communicating brand mission, vision and values source

in disseminating them through the organisation.' When asked about the internal barriers to realising the full potential of the brand, the interviewees cite a whole range of factors, but several of them can be grouped together under a lack of clarity and a failure to communicate (lack of clarity in what the brand stands for, decentralization/emphasis on local identity, weaknesses in the internal communications function, differentiating between corporate and consumer brands, too fragmented).[19]

One of the key conclusions of the research is that there needs to be more leadership in the articulation and communication of branding to the widest possible audience. The strongest brands are those that consistently live up to their brand promise: 'their employees work in strong corporate cultures where what the brand stands for is universally understood and every aspect of the organisation is galvanised to ensure its successful delivery.' ORC's findings are also backed up by other studies.

Similarly, while the evidence for the benefits of empowerment is persuasive, research shows that the ideal can be removed from the reality. For example, the 1997 British Social Attitudes survey looked at the attitudes of people towards work and found their main concerns focused on the absence of empowerment (unfair managers and lacking a voice) and the failures of internal communication. A study by the Institute of Social Research of 400 companies in 17 countries among 8 million workers found falls in the levels of

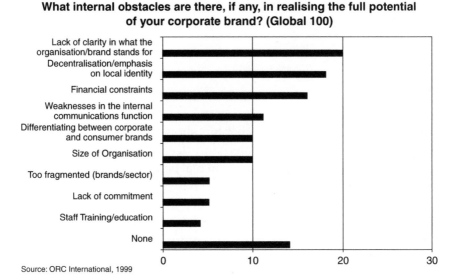

What internal obstacles are there, if any, in realising the full potential of your corporate brand? (Global 100)

Source: ORC International, 1999

Figure 4.5 Obstacles to realizing brand potential

employee satisfaction – the most pronounced of any European country was Britain, where ratings fell 11 percentage points over a 10-year period. A 1995 study into quality circles and problem solving groups in the United Kingdom found that no more than 2 per cent of all organizations with more than 25 workers used them.[20]

Intellectually, leaders often seem to recognize the benefit of building an organizational purpose to which everyone can relate, it seems obvious from the research that many struggle to deliver it. Although organizational structures and cultures can get in the way, the fundamental barrier is more to do with attitude. Leaders have to believe that vision and values can only make a difference if they acquire real meaning. They have to move beyond words into action and to engage employees at an emotional level. Too many organizations go through the process of articulating and talking about values without making them relevant to people. There is little benefit to the nicely framed and well written brand statement if it remains something that people decorate their walls with rather than live in their day-to-day lives. As Warren Bennis says:

What effective leaders are going to have to do is create not just a vision, but a vision with meaning…The vision has to be shared. And the only way that it can be shared is for it to have meaning for the people who are involved in it.[21]

Summary

Taken together, these last two chapters show that employees want to engage with a clearly articulated and deeply motivating sense of purpose and that employers can gain real benefits by understanding and meeting those needs. For this to happen, the process of managing people has to move from abstraction to a focus on a humanistic method that stresses genuine empowerment. Some organizations have already made this journey, but others find it difficult to make the transition. As organizations grow, the difficulties increase. It is far easier for managers of a small organization to understand and empathize with employees. People are closer and the relationship is more personalized. Take an organization of 100,000 people and management can never know the individuals. This encourages employers to move boxes around organizational charts, to re-engineer and restructure without fully addressing the human consequences. This leads to those public and employee relations disasters that can befall large organizations – where sitting on the outside you wonder how could they have been so insensitive and stupid?

Thus the next chapters look at how organizations can both articulate and give meaning to their brands. To move away from the abstract to the concrete.

Notes

1 Rajan, Amin (2000) Leadership in the knowledge age, *RSA Journal*, **2** (4), p 61.
2 Hegel, Georg Wihelm Friedrich (1999) *The Philosophy of History*, Prometheus Books.
3 Taylor AJP (1995) *From the Boer War to the Cold War*, Hamish Hamilton, London, p 124.

4   Godin, Seth (2000) Unleash your ideavirus, *Fast Company*, (August), p 122

5   Edvinsson, Leif and Malone, Michael (1997) *Intellectual Capital: The proven way to establish your company's real value by measuring its hidden brainpower*, Piatkus, London, p 11.

6   Edvinsson, Leif and Malone, Michael (1997) *Intellectual Capital: The proven way to establish your company's real value by measuring its hidden brainpower*, Piatkus, London, p 22.

7   Gyllenhammer Pehr (1977) *People at Work*, Addison Wesley, London, p 18.

8   Brown, John Seeley and Duguid, Paul (2000) Balancing act: how to capture knowledge without killing it, *Harvard Business Review*, (May-June), p 79.

9   Maslow, Abraham (1998) *Maslow on Management*, Wiley, Chichester, p 51.

10 Pfeffer, Jeffrey (1998) *The Human Equation*, Harvard Business School Press, Boston, MA, pp 46–47.

11 Dufficy, Martin (1998) The empowerment audit – measured improvement, *Industrial and Commercial Training*, 30 (4), pp 142–46.

12 Hamel, Gary (2000) Reinvent your company, *Fortune*, **141** (12) (June 12), p 112.

13 Virgin Atlantic also recognize this. Their brand book states under the heading 'An obsessive attention to detail': 'Everything we do should be characterised by an obsessive and uncompromising attention to detail. We all know that any journey is made up of many little experiences and that it doesn't take much to turn a happy traveller into an unhappy one. We cannot afford this and we must not let it happen.'

14 Collins, James and Porras, Jerry (1998) *Built to Last: Successful habits of visionary companies*, Random House Business Books, London.

15 Aksel Sandemose's *A Fugitive Crosses His Tracks* was published in 1933 and is set in a mythical place called Jante, which has its own law that dictates social and moral standards.

16 Dutton, Jane and Dukerich, Janet (1991) Keeping an eye on the mirror: image and identity in organizational adaptation, *Academy of Management Journal*, **34** (3), pp 517–54.

17 Dutton, Jane and Dukerich, Janet (1991) Keeping an eye on the mirror: image and identity in organizational adaptation, *Academy of Management Journal*, **34** (3), p 517–54, at p 548.

18 A 1998 study by MORI, commissioned by MCA, into 350 managers and staff in British companies showed that 37 per cent of people are champions (know what they need to do and are committed to delivering), but 39 per cent are weak links (switched off – lack understanding and commitment), 14 per cent are loose cannons (committed to goals but lack the understanding necessary to deliver) and 10 per cent are bystanders (know what they need to do, but lack commitment to organizational goals).

19 Opinion Research Corporation International (1999) *Global 100 – Attitudes to Corporate Branding, Opinion Research Corporation*. ORC International repeated the research in 2000 among 250 companies. The overall figure for 'the brand mission, vision and values are understood by all employees, most of whom believe in them strongly' showed an increase from 47 per cent to 51 per cent.

20 Pfeffer, Jeffrey (1998) *The Human Equation*, Harvard Business School Press, p 62.

21 Bennis, Warren (1997) Becoming a leader of leaders, in Gibson, R (ed) *Rethinking the Future*, Nicholas Brealy Publishing, p 156.

five

Defining **the brand**

The previous chapters have outlined the importance of employees living the brand in their day to day roles. This and subsequent chapters will look at how organizations can define, embed, manage and evaluate their brands over time. Each of these stages is important if a brand is to engage all the employees in an organization. A brand can only truly come to life if it enters the collective psyche of the organization and thus becomes intuitive to people. The employees of a strong brand, such as Patagonia, do not need to consult the brand definition every time they have to make a decision. They tend to know what is right for them. This factor contains an important truth for the brand-definition process. If the words used to define a brand are not authentic to the organization they will never become intuitive. Intuition can only occur when the brand is an accurate reflection of what people believe. Thus defining a brand is a search for truth.

A search for truth

All organizations have a purpose, a vision and a set of values. Just think of the simplest start-up: two people, an office, telephones and computers. Why does this start-up exist? Perhaps it is a wireless company that is going to provide tracking devices for vehicles. Car companies would insert the tracker into the engine compartment and then if the car is stolen its position can be tracked via any hand held device or computer. So the *purpose* of the company is to help provide car owners with greater piece of mind.

The *vision* is a sense of the future in which any object of value from computers to cargoes can be tracked at minimal cost. The values might be built around such ideas as honesty, innovation, partnership and professionalism. These *values* are what our two would-be entrepreneurs believe to be important for them to succeed. They know that they have to think innovatively and to develop innovative products that keep them ahead of competitors. They recognize that they will have to act as partners to the car companies and perhaps insurers to build acceptance for their idea. They want to stress that they will always act professionally and they believe that the way to build a business is to be honest about their knowledge and capabilities. Perhaps if they have grand ambitions to be a billion dollar company in their first two years, they will think through their purpose and vision and values at the very beginning and write them down, but if they're like most start-ups they won't. It simply won't be a priority. Yet, here's how Chris Lochhead of Scient responds to the question, 'what's the most important thing about your vision and values?'

> I think getting clear on them early and then communicating and reinforcing them relentlessly. The last part, is the CEO and the rest of the management team has to live them. Otherwise it's absolute garbage. The thing I love about Scient is it's real. I think Bob Howe [chief executive], gets a lot of credit for it: that everybody early on shared the vision, we figured how to articulate it, we got very clear on what the values meant and we've embedded it in the culture. You see it in our e-mails, we talk about it all the time, there are posters up all over the place. It's very vivid in the Scient culture.

However, Scient is probably a rarity. Entrepreneurs look at a business environment and see a gap or an opportunity to do something different. They then structure a business concept based around their perception of what the market wants, their skills and knowledge and the underlying beliefs they have about a way of being. We can equate these ideas and beliefs to the purpose, mission and values, but the entrepreneur will probably not define them until later on. It took Patagonia 30 years to move from a generalized understanding of what the brand was about to a more formalized definition of it and it took Adobe 17 years.

Generally, the driver for defining values is organizational growth. While a founder or founders can influence a small to medium sized organization personally, a growth in numbers and/or locations makes it ever more difficult to sustain that influence. The ideas of the founder become less pronounced and subsets of vision and values start to emerge within other parts of the organization. This tends to lead to a lack of consistency in the presentation of the organization and consequently a lack of continuity of experience for customers. Poor clarity in the external image is frequently a catalyst for embarking on a branding programme. This inconsistency is often exacerbated if the founder leaves or the company merges with others. The brand idea can be the glue that holds the parts together. This does not create a world of rulebooks but rather a common set of ideas that can steer attitudes and behaviour. The assumptions and values that guided the founders and their decisions, can, if they are credible and well articulated, become the assumptions and values of employees. In the longer term the brand idea is something that should develop an independent existence. Senior executives should be able to influence the brand, but its essence should transcend the coming and going of people. Melissa Dyrdahl of Adobe says:

> The values have always been there and as a small company it's very easy to have them be much more a part of the company through oral history than anything; through John and Chuck [the founders] setting the example. But over the years as the company has grown to 3,000 employees worldwide it's not possible for everyone to have that connection with John and Chuck and to witness the values and standards.

The underlying question here is, does the organization need to formally articulate its values? For example, the highly successful UK-based travel agency, Trailfinders, which was started in 1970 in London, by Mike Gooley, an ex-SAS soldier, has never articulated its values, yet certain ideas based on customer service are pervasive in the organization. There are probably many other exceptions. If the values are truly felt and lived, without them being written down, then employees can quite effectively live the brand. But without the reference point of a statement, the danger of subversion is always higher. Imagine if Shakespeare's actor friends had not gathered his plays into the First Folio after his death. We would have to rely on an oral tradition for the content. Over time different interpretations and the vagaries of memory would have led to alternative presentations. No one would now be able to define the ideas and the meaning of the works. This variability might be quite exciting, but the written text is of itself not constraining. The power of Shakespeare is that the underlying ideas allow for wide interpretation without losing the central vision. The Director, Akira Kurosawa, can reinterpret *King Lear* in the tradition of the Samurai in *Ran*, while Sir Ian McKellen can present *Richard III* in a 1930s Fascist context and Baz Luhrmann can show the star-cross'd lovers Romeo and Juliet in an MTV style Hong Kong action movie set in present day America. The Shakespearean vision stimulates the imagination and encourages adaptation. This is because the aspectuality of truth (its lack of singularity), which is rather a 20th-century idea, is fundamental to the 16th-century Shakespearean work. In a business context this means that the founder's vision will be true for the founder but will be subject to different interpretations by others over time. It will never be possible to produce a set of ideas or words that have the same meaning and resonance for everyone. Indeed part of the vitality of a good brand definition is that it does more than maintain existing behaviour. It should inspire people to discover new ways of doing things. Patagonia's commitment to quality and environmentalism, Nike's passion for sporting excellence and SAS Airlines' belief in Scandinavianness and friendly informality do not restrict innovation. These brand ideas provide the focus for people to imagine how to deliver them in new ways. These companies, and others, need their Kurosawas and their Luhrmanns; people who want to extend and experiment with the meaning of the brand, while still maintaining its essence. Like many a successful brand manager, Luhrmann may provide a completely new presentation for *Romeo and Juliet*, but he does not change the core idea of the power of love and the hubris of the lovers' families.

The danger in writing down the meaning of the brand and articulating the vision and values is that people can sometime believe the job is done. The brand is there for all to see. Yet writing down a set of words does not create meaning. As the Shakespearean analogy suggests, the layers of meaning appear through repetition and exploration. Yet so many organizations (as the ORC research in the previous chapter indicated) never move beyond pinning words up on a wall or sending round a booklet that lists the words that are meant to define the brand.

The definition process

The world of branding is awash with models. Is this because of the aspectuality of truth? Perhaps, but, there are two fundamental problems with most of the models. First, they tend to be overly complex, both in terms of structure and language. The real value of a model ought to be in the simplification of a complicated idea. Second, a model should be usable. For a professional marketing audience this doesn't necessarily equate to simplification, but in an organizational context a fundamental aspect is that, whatever their role in the organization, employees should be able to understand and use the brand – otherwise how can they live it?

Two anecdotes make this point. First, a major UK insurance company, which had undergone the process of articulating its brand produced a thick ring-bound folder on the brand that even the corporate communications director confessed to not understanding. Second, a global charity that employed the services of an advertising agency to define its brand found itself confronted with a vast array of words to describe the various facets of the brand: 12 brand profile words, six brand personality traits and several paragraphs on the mission and vision. This was despite the fact that one of the current national definitions of the brand was found to be ignored by staff because it was too complex.

Rather than focusing overtly on a model it is more valuable to concentrate on the process of brand definition. If the ultimate goal is to gain organization-wide commitment to the idea, then this should be the primary process. In a start-up organization, it will probably be the founders and perhaps partner organizations that sit down and discuss the purpose of the organization. The simple objective here ought to be to create something that is appropriate for the organization and helps it to meet its long-term goals. In well-established businesses, which need to formulate their brands for the first time or perhaps review an existing definition, the goal should be to construct a methodology that is participative. This runs counter to the approach adopted by many in both the public and private sector. In many instances, brand ideas – the vision and values – are generated by senior managers, often with a communication and marketing background. A working group is put together, market research may be commissioned, consultants employed, workshops conducted and the words crafted by a writer. However well constructed, this is still a top down exercise. It is the recommended process of some writers who view the internal marketing of a brand idea as essentially an advertising task. The failing here is twofold. First, if genuine commitment is to be achieved among employees, the brand idea has to touch the core of why people work for the organization. It is not something that can necessarily be crafted, although the better phrased it is the better, rather it is something that has to be discovered. Second, the views of managers, may not be an accurate reflection of the organization. As Cees van Riel states:

> This method measures in the first instance the picture that the managers have of their company, which is not necessarily the same as the view of the company held by other employees or members of target groups.[1]

Having attempted to help organizations define and embed both top down and participative brand ideas, I can vouch for the latter as the more effective method. There are also some interesting examples of organizations that have developed effective bottom-up participative approaches to projects:

Shell

In 1997, Shell started to emphasize its commitment to sustainable development and the environment and in 1998 it published its first social report. Inspired by these initiatives a Shell employee felt that although the intent was good, there was a gap between the idea and the reality. To close the gap, he came up with the idea of working in partnership with globally oriented non-governmental organizations (NGOs). The question was how to turn this idea into a programme. Using the company intranet to create a discussion forum, like-minded individuals got in contact and a project team was formed for what became known as Project Better World. Initially it was hard to find supporters among middle management but more senior managers were supportive. The real change in attitude came when chairman, Mark Moody-Stuart, put his weight behind the idea and wrote a piece for the first edition of a newsletter. This gave the team real legitimacy, which helped to deliver funding for the project. By the end of 1999 the team had developed partnerships with VSO (Voluntary Service Overseas) and Earthwatch and had sent 34 people off to work with these organizations. Enabled by the intranet, other parts of the Shell network became involved and the scheme began to generate a momentum of its own with people from all over the world working on links and projects with NGOs. None of this was centrally planned – the commitment and success has come from committed individuals who believed that by working together they could create something powerful and beneficial to Shell. As Shelley Wheeler, the first convert to the programme says: 'The key benefits for Shell are developing its staff, developing its relationships with stakeholders and recognising that this can help change the culture (of Shell).'

Dutch Ministry of Transport

Like many transport departments around the world, the Dutch Ministry of Transport found itself having problems making decisions on large infrastructure projects such as high-speed trains, major highways and the extension of the airport. The population density of the Netherlands compounded the difficulty of reaching agreements. A small case in point typified the problem. The Minister for Transport, Hanja Maij-Weggen, tried to persuade parliament that the hard shoulder should be used when the roads were busy to ease traffic congestion. However, there were concerns about safety and the suggestion was rejected. To try to resolve the dilemma about congestion, the democratic idea of a public consultation exercise on Dutch roads was instituted. In many countries this would equate to years of inaction. However, the Dutch made this participative exercise work. The consultation exercise was undertaken by an internal consultancy that Maij-Weggen initiated, called Infralab. The group, which was staffed by seconded personnel, started by outlining the objectives and the consultation process to the public and transport professionals that were going to participate in the discussions. Peter Vroom of the consultancy, QM Communicatie, who worked on some of the communication aspects of the project says:

> The main factor in being successful was that people knew what kind of process they were getting involved in. It wasn't open-ended. People knew when they started in the process that they were going to survey the problems now and that within a month there would be solution…You have to be clear about the rules. It must lead to a decision.

Infralab asked people to talk about the problems associated with driving. This information was clustered and condensed into five or so key issues. People were then asked about the solutions, which were again clustered. Without prompting one of the suggestions was to use the hard shoulder in peak traffic times. Although the solution now had the weight of the public consultation behind it, the Minister opted to conduct an experiment to prove the validity of the idea. A small section of road that suffered from particularly bad traffic was selected and tests run. The safety fears seemed to be unfounded and congestion was eased. Peter Vroom adds:

> It was the process that was different – the political process and the way people were involved with it, made it acceptable. It was the result of hundreds of volunteers. People felt they were involved with something exciting.

Once the principle of participation was shown to be successful, it came to be a defining methodology for decision making within the Ministry. Maij-Weggen's three ministerial successors have all supported the Infralab system, which has evolved into an ongoing innovation programme called Roads to the Future. Although it is a challenge to remain innovative, both in process and content, one of the key benefits is that decisions on transport have been made more quickly, rather than slowing things up, as some critics of participative decision-making argued. Part of the reason for this was that a clear timetable was set up and maintained. It hints at one of the key factors in effective brand programmes: maintaining momentum and ensuring that people can see the impact of their contributions, while their interest levels are high. Allow the process to drift and disenchantment can soon set in.

SAS

On 7 May 2000, SAS Airlines launched their new corporate identity to the outside world. It comprised of a new look to the planes, to the staff uniform, to literature and to the food. However, underlying this new look was a participative approach to generating meaning for the brand idea. The essence of the brand was based on a specific Scandinavian notion of informal elegance. To unearth the real meaning of this idea, which had been derived through research with passengers and employees, the staff were asked to think through how they would deliver it. All staff had an input into the project. Their view was that informal elegance was almost like when you're at home with friends. For cabin crews this suggested a certain tone to personal communications and an allowance for passengers to be treated in different ways as individuals – as you would with friends. The idea was then carried through into other aspects of the presentation of the brand. Customers can buy a ticket for any airline from the SAS Web site. The staff managing the Web project felt that friends would do that bit extra for each other and that the Web should reflect this thought. When it came to the uniforms, the cabin crew worked with the designer to create clothes that reflected the brand idea and that they would enjoy wearing. Robert Lilja, who worked on the project when he was a manager with SAS, says that employee involvement was an essential part of the process: 'If you want people to do something they must want to do it. The brand project created the willingness among employees to want to do things. During the process people discovered that they wanted to change.'

As SAS and the Dutch roads programme shows, if participation is to work it has to be genuine. The role of the consultant should be to facilitate the involvement of the participants.

Consultancies can provide an important service in defining brands. They have research skills, they can be objective, they can encourage employees to say things that they would be unwilling to discuss with colleagues and they can lend authority to the process. Yet, they should not define the brand idea itself, they should not present the idea to employees and they should not claim the vision and values as their own creation. This should be an exercise in humility. One of the best accolades I received having worked as a consultant for the charity VSO for some eighteen months on their brand definition was someone telling me subsequently that the process had been done internally without the help of any consultants. Matthew Bell of VSO says:

> People use consultants too much – not in the sense of too often, but rather too thoroughly. Creative solutions, for instance, may get much greater buy-in, if they're developed in-house. And brand values have to be generated by the people who will be asked to live them. When we defined the concepts behind the VSO brand, we used consultants to facilitate the process, but not to refine the ideas themselves.

Brand education

Before launching into a brand definition process the first decision is whether to call the output a brand. The word 'brand' has many different interpretations. The most obvious associations for people unconnected with branding are the brands they see in supermarkets and the clothing brands they buy in shops. Brand is also applied in increasingly diverse ways. Governments, politicians, newspapers and pop stars are referred to as 'brands'. The media and design consultancies also refer to logos as 'brands'. There is an overwhelming tendency to think of the visual representation of a product or service as the brand. This encourages some to think of brands as something superficial that is specifically the remit of the marketing or communications department. However, as has been argued in this and other books, brands only properly exist in the minds of consumers and represent the totality of experience. Thus the brand is as much about internal understanding as external communications. The logo is only the tip of the iceberg. The result of this confusion about branding is that the announcement of a branding programme can be met by a sea of employee cynicism and the assumption that a logo change is imminent or a new advertising campaign is about to be launched. How should this problem be tackled? Some organizations decide that the 'brand' word should be avoided and that it is better to talk about the organizational mission, vision and values. This tends to lead to verbal gymnastics in an attempt to describe the thing that is being defined, but nonetheless it can be more comfortable for employees. In particular, talking about brands can be uncomfortable in non-profit or governmental organizations. There is a view that brands are the province of the commercial world and do not sit comfortably with the idea of what a government department or charity exists to do. The alternative to avoiding the brand word is to embrace it and then first to educate employees as to its meaning and then to reinforce its value through a consistent emphasis on its value to the organization. Although charities can be reticent about the brand idea, VSO decided that it wanted to create a more commercial attitude within the organization and deliberately set out to promote branding. To do this it conducted a series of branding orientation workshops, led by its communications director, where people from across the organization came together to look at brands in non-traditional contexts. The idea was to educate people that brands were not just things that sat on supermarket shelves but could be applied to charities. The groups looked at the factors that made brands strong and the benefits that could accrue. The process not only familiarized employees with the terminology of branding and marketing – it encouraged a more appropriate idea of the scope of the process. By investing this time at the outset, it helped to achieve a positive attitude, enhanced the effectiveness of the subsequent research and built organization-wide support. Of course, if the organizational environment is such that people already seem to have a sophisticated understanding of branding then the education programme can be ignored. This is rare. Mostly organizations eschew this front-end process because of the time and cost involved. Yet it should be seen as an investment. The solution is more robust and the potential commitment is higher.

An integrated approach

Although complex models should be avoided when talking to employees, it is valuable for the instigators of the brand programme to understand how the brand idea relates to the overall formulation of identity and image. Over the years much work has been done on this by a number of writers. One of the recent constructs is by Maria Chiara Riondino of Accenture (formerly Andersen Consulting). She took models developed by such writers as Kennedy, Abratt and Stuart and then researched their ideas with a number of organizations. Her evolution of their ideas is shown in Figure 5.1.

The model demonstrates several important facets of how branding works:

- The identity of an organization is formed by its personality, culture, philosophy, values and mission. This is the core of what an organization is.
- The identity is transmitted outwards by the 'brand idea', which is the articulation of the unique attributes that make the organization what it is. The formulation of the 'brand idea' can take different forms, as examples in this book will show, but the important aspect is its truth; that it is defined by the identity.
- The 'brand idea' is itself communicated through three key mechanisms: the nature of marketing communications, employees' interpretations of the identity and the nature of the products and services. Although only one of these three boxes specifically mentions employees, the point to note is that products, services and marketing communications are created by and delivered by employees. This hints at the importance of integrating all aspects of the organization's systems and processes so that there is a unity in the way the brand is presented.
- The three boxes all interrelate with each other, which stresses the overarching role of employees and also indicates the importance of internally marketing, external marketing communcations. Employees will not be able to support advertising or public relations messages if they do not understand them.
- As well as the planned communications of the organization, unplanned communications are also transmitted. These 'moments

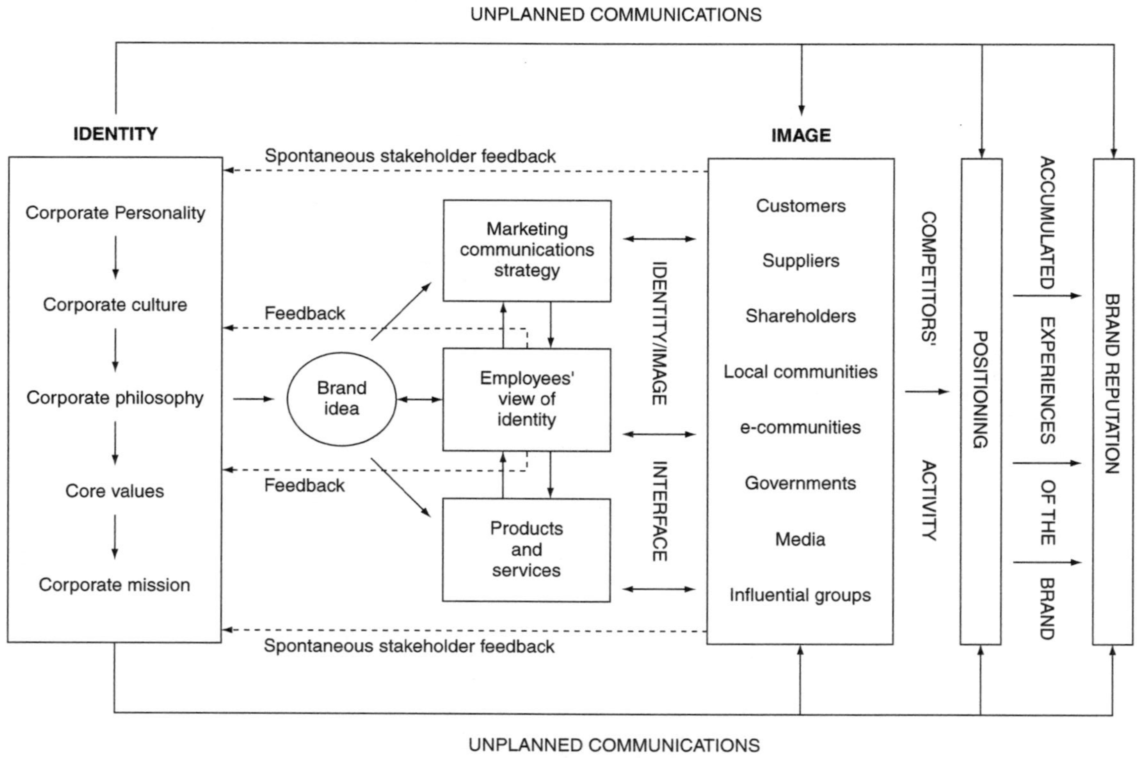

Figure 5.1 The Brand model

of truth' are again determined by the identity and employees' understanding of the brand idea.

- The goal is to create an appropriate and effective image among a variety of stakeholders, which over time creates a reputation for the organization.
- There is ongoing feedback to the organization. The image and reputation impacts on the identity and the way that employees see themselves. As Hatch and Schultz note: 'insofar as organizational members encounter organizational images as part of their lives both inside and outside the organization, it is likely there will be feedback from image to identity.'[2]
- The interface between identity and image is seamless, partly because of the advent of the Web. The two-way flows indicate that the barriers that used to exist between the organization and its audiences have broken down and that there is more direct interaction. With the advent of more effective CRM systems, people within the organization know more about customers than ever before and as a result can deliver more personalized communications and products. Equally the development of extranets enables more effective communities of interest with professional audiences, such as buyers and suppliers.

Although we tend to read the chart from left to right, the number of leftward flowing arrows suggests the growing importance of pull factors. Organizations still spend large amounts of money on pushing out messages but the growing sophistication of software enables the various audiences to pull the information and products and services they need from the organization.

The model sets the scene for the necessary research methodology, because it puts the focus on people and the need for a clearly defined brand idea that engages employees and creates the right sort of image with the relevant audiences.

Conducting research

Using the Riondino model we should recognize that the starting point for articulating the brand is to really understand the organization's identity. This is the role of research. The brand research should be as broadly based as possible. There are two reasons for this. First, it is important that the brand works for everyone in the organization. In a professional services firm the brand not only needs to work for the consultants but also the support staff. In an international organization, the brand needs to work for all countries, not just the head office. If the research base is narrow the danger is that the needs of some groups will be ignored. In turn they will ignore the brand, believing it has no relevance for them. Second, the research can also be educative and build consensus. The process itself is cathartic. It gives people the time and the opportunity to analyse the organization and how they feel about it. This is especially important for the cynics and the potential saboteurs.[3] Every organization will have these people: the ones that have seen these initiatives before and are convinced they will not work or believe that branding is irrelevant to the organization. Rather than ignoring these people it is better to engage them. Letting them have their say will not necessarily ensure their active support but it provides the opportunity to persuade.

The research itself should encompass three elements:

- desk research;
- employee research;
- external research.

Desk research

Companies, especially those with long histories, contain a wealth of information that provide clues as to their ideas and values. Sometimes there are even books or documented histories about the organization. Before embarking on original research it is always valuable to review what already exists. This has the benefit of providing insights into how the organization behaves at key moments and hinting at the assumptions that guide the organization and that can be questioned during subsequent interviews. As well as the documentation it is also valuable to observe the architecture of buildings, the layout of offices, the descriptors of the organization, the language people use, the organizational structures, the methodologies in use and the tone and style of communications material. These are what the writer Edgar Schein calls the artifacts and creations of the organization, which are the expressions of the values and the basic assumptions. It is not always possible to decipher these artifacts just by looking at them and one has to be cautious about the truth of the artifacts. Just because an organization employs an open-plan office layout this cannot be read as a belief in organizational egalitarianism. It simply may be a functional solution or a desired idea rather than true. If, however, the organization eschews individual titles, provides exactly the same square footage for everyone whatever their position, has one common eating area, provides share options for everyone and has an open-plan office, there may be more substance to the view. It is the same when we go to other people's houses for the first time. We begin to form a picture from the individual elements and then as we see the totality of the home we form a judgement as to the value set of the individual. This may or may not be borne out by the reality of experience. We might find that the person is trying to convey an idea of himself or herself as an aesthete, but find out that he or she has no real knowledge of aesthetics. We then see the dissonance. Equally with an organization: one might review the approach to advertising and come away with a picture of innovation, only to discover the opposite.

Thus the desk research phase should be cumulative and should help to pose questions rather than supply answers. For example, if it uncovers in the company newsletter that there is considerable emphasis given to the success of the sales team and that the bonus scheme favours these people, the immediate conclusion ought not to be that this is a sales-focused organization. Rather it should lead to a questioning in the primary research that asks whether this is indeed the case and, if so, why.

Employee research

Employee research can involve both quantitative and qualitative methods. The objective is to try to uncover the organizational values – the things that matter most to people and steer decision making. The difficulty is that values are not always obvious. Office conversations rarely focus on the values. People do not stand at the coffee machine debating whether the most important value is 'challenging' or 'integrity.' However, they do discuss stories, events and actions that express the values. They do debate how the chief executive reacted to criticisms from the environmental lobby. They may even talk about some past event that expresses the organization's beliefs. An example of this is an advertising agency I once worked for. This organization's biggest client was a major tea brand. The agency was renowned in its time for developing highly distinctive and memorable advertising for such clients as Zanussi, Homepride Flour, Access and L'Oreal. Following much research the agency presented an animated television campaign. The client was unmoved and rejected the work completely. The client disliked the animation and the character designed to represent the brand. The agency faced a dilemma. It believed it had created an effective and long-term idea for the brand and yet the client wouldn't agree to it. The agency re-presented the idea, but the client was insistent and told the agency to start again. The agency response was to resign the account. This decision entered the agency's folklore. It said to every employee that creativity and integrity mattered. It also said implicitly that if you got into a confrontation with a client and your thinking was seen to be right then you would be fully supported. That one decision to resign the agency's largest client represented for everyone in the agency one of the reasons why they worked there.

Research methods

As values can be subtle, it does suggest that overall the most appropriate form of research is qualitative. The open-ended nature of the research enables the analyst to probe in depth the cultural background of the organization and to unearth the assumptions that underpin the values. Although there is no one right way to conduct this research, an approach that has proven to be effective is *one-to-one interviews with senior managers* to determine their perceptions of the organization, beliefs about its culture, the defining events in its history, its role in the world and its future position. The objective is to understand the historical context, the current situation and future intentions. The historical context can be particularly illuminating as organizations can sometimes find themselves slaves of the past: the case with such prominent British retailers as Marks & Spencer and J Sainsbury. Each of these had a long and successful history and a distinctive view of conducting business, but each ran into difficult times at the end of the 1990s, because the dead weight of tradition seemed to stifle change. Alternatively, organizations change direction and seem keen to escape their past. This can prove hard for organizations with well-entrenched images as it may take years to move people's perceptions. However, the very act of change and the emphasis on escaping the past can be instructive as to the values for the future. The number of one-to-one interviews will vary, but it should include the 'difficult' people and the key executives of the organization.

Discussion groups with staff can uncover their understanding of the organization. The composition of the groups depends on the organization's culture. If the culture encourages the free flow of ideas, then people from different levels of the organization can be mixed together. If it is more hierarchical, then greater attention needs to be paid to getting people of a similar level. The rationale of this is simply that people may be worried about saying what they really think in the company of senior people. Whereas it may be difficult to mix people of different status, it is valuable to mix people from different backgrounds. This helps to generate a more complete idea of the organization and its purpose.

Generally the group discussions can be longer than consumer groups. This seems to work because whereas consumer interest often wanes after almost one hour, employees almost invariably seize upon the chance to have their say. Therefore, these groups can comfortably extend to an hour-and-a-half to two hours. Working to a discussion guide, the following broad topics can be covered:

- Understanding of the organization's purpose and direction: how well people can articulate what the organization exists to do and whether there is clarity about the future.
- Resources and tools to implement direction: even when people know where they are meant to be heading they do not always feel they have the resources or the skills to get them there. Thus, this tests the current validity of the vision and values and the propensity of people to fulfil them in the future.

- Resource and skills gaps: these relate to the dissonance that may exist between where the organization wants to be and where people feel they are now.
- Organizational values overall and variances by area: as well as ascertaining what people believe the current values to be for the organization – ideally supported by stories to show the values in action – different departments may have different values. The research needs to check whether the business unit or area values support the overall or undermine it.
- Use of the values in peoples' day-to-day jobs: emphasizing values only makes sense if people can see how to use the values in their everyday work. For example, is it clear to the receptionist or the finance department how they can be innovative, professional, inspired and challenging (or whatever the values may be)?
- Current barriers to the effective understanding of values: there are often internal barriers to understanding the values, such as the failure of management to communicate them.
- Quality of internal communication: the effectiveness of internal communication is a strong indicator of the values, because values only really come to life when they are communicated. The moderator should probe upward, downward and horizontal mechanisms.
- Perception of current image and impact of image on employees: how employees perceive the external image of the organization is important for their own self-esteem and the strength of the bond they feel for the organization. It also pinpoints a potential barrier in that a negative external image may inhibit interest in the values.
- The ideal image: no holds barred – how would people like to be seen by the outside world and what would it take to get there and to stay there.

The group should not just be encouraged to be descriptive. At each key point the moderator should asking 'why do you think that?' and probe for examples. To provoke a response, stimulus material can also be introduced in the form of literature, advertising and films. At the end of the discussion the group can also be asked to do something involving participation. Two suggestions are mood boards and scenarios. Both are designed to encourage people to think more laterally about the issues they have been discussing. For mood boards, the group should be supplied with an eclectic mix of photographs and words and asked to put together a collage of the brand. For example, when this exercise was conducted with the Worldwide Fund for Nature/World Wildlife Fund (WWF) the interesting aspect of the collages was the limited emphasis given to animals and the greater emphasis on pollution, people and the environment. The insight into the brand is that although animal imagery is used extensively in fund raising, the people who work for WWF recognize that it is impossible to ring fence endangered species and that you have to deal with the larger human and environmental context in which they live. The other method is creating scenarios: asking people to create a verbal and visual storyline about the brand. The value of this is that it encourages people to think about how consumers and other audiences interact with the brand in their day to day lives.

Laddering

An alternative methodology to that described above is to use laddering techniques. If one could analyse all the actions of individuals within an organization, it would be possible to decode the underlying ideas. However, this is difficult in practical terms. Instead, through interviews with employees one can uncover the underlying ideas that cause the actions. Work in the Netherlands by Van Rekom[4] in the area helps to indicate the degree to which people identify with the organization's cause, their degree of empowerment – their willingness to go beyond the rulebook and their ability to relate their role to the rest of the organization. The laddering methodology starts with the following four questions:

   What is your job?
   What exactly do you do?
   Why do you do it in this way?
   Why is that important?

The interviewer can then repeat the process by asking about the specifics of a particular task and then again probing the underlying rationale for the action. Thus if we asked retail assistants what they do when they receive a complaint from a customer, they might say 'I have to find a supervisor who will either deal with the problem or give me the authority to deal with it.' We might then ask, 'why do you do that?' The reply might be: 'well, company rules are very specific. We're not allowed to deal with complaints directly.' The final question would then be: 'Why is that important?' The response then might be: 'We've been told that dealing with customer complaints is very important, so the company wants to keep a record. We involve supervisors, because we think it makes the customer feel their complaint is being taken seriously.' At each stage in the process the interviewer should encourage the respondent to confirm the interpretation of the statement, by saying 'so what you mean is...' or 'the picture you create is...'. This ensures that the full meaning of a statement is uncovered. This complaints process is far removed from the empowering world of Nordstrom, but if the findings of this interview are replicated with others we might judge that:

- complaints are taken seriously;
- the company is customer focused;
- the company tracks its performance;
- communications are instructional, but people know what is expected of them;
- the company does not empower its employees in this area.

Thus from focusing on the actions of individuals we gain a picture of the values as understood by employees. Van Rekom also recommends that the findings of the interviews be integrated into a quantitative phase of research, which can test, whether the findings of the laddering are replicated throughout the organization. The final picture that emerges from this process is an understanding of the organization's purpose and values and the purpose and values of individual groups or teams. This internal picture can also be compared to the external image that customers and other audiences have of the organization. One of the benefits of conducting this quantitative analysis prior to a brand programme, is that it sets up a benchmark against which future progress can be measured.

External research

Vision and values are driven primarily by a sense of what the organization believes to be true. Consequently the process is about creating internal understanding. However, without the input of external research there is a danger of creating a brand idea that has great power internally, but is irrelevant when expressed externally through written or personal communications. To guard against this and to ensure that the brand will have resonance with others, the organization needs to acquire insight into how others see it. The complexity here is that there may be a great variety of audiences: government, media, advisors, suppliers, buyers, industry commentators, local communities. Although one can prioritize the audiences that are most important, potentially each audience needs to be covered. The method for reaching these audiences can vary. It can involve questionnaires, telephone interviews or face-to-face interviews. The research should aim to uncover:

- people's relationship with the organization: how they first came into contact with it and how they have interacted with it over time;
- quality of relationship: overall has the experience been positive or negative – stories to substantiate claims;
- belief about organizational direction: where they believe the organization is placing its emphasis now and in the future;
- strength of values: what beliefs seem to emanate from the organization and how consistently and clearly these are communicated;
- mindspace: how important the organization is to them – how they see the organization relative to others;
- industry discriminators: what is important within their business area – how well does the organization perform against those discriminators;
- communication: frequency and quality;
- the future: the dynamics they believe will be important in the future and how well the organization is positioned to take advantage of changes.

Using the research

Making sense of the research is concerned with picking out the key strands that emerge from the content. However, this should not be the sole responsibility of a consultant or researcher. If the use of the research is to be genuinely participative it should be shared with as wide an audience as possible. This is sometimes difficult for organizations to accept. Market research is traditionally seen as something that managers commission and use. However, empowerment, as observed earlier, means the diminution of a manager's power and its take-up by others. This is not beneficial because being democratic feels good but rather because the greater the breadth and depth of engagement, the greater the likelihood of subsequent commitment to the output. Deciding on the best way of sharing will be in part defined by the culture of the organization and will need to balance what is desirable and what is practicable.

At this stage it is too unwieldy to engage everyone in the creative process of articulating the brand. The best solution is to ask people to volunteer to form a creative group that will define the brand. This group can be anything from 5 to 20 people. The goal is to construct a group that is representative of the organization. Therefore, all the different departments and functions should have an individual involved with the development of the brand.

Although the group can choose its own working methodology it needs some points of accountability. How should the brand be defined? In the past I have given people examples of other good brands and suggested the group chooses whichever structure feels most appropriate. In other instances I have suggested a structure. There are several different ways of constructing a brand and no doubt each organization would argue for the validity of its own framework. Organizations talk variously about credo, purpose, vision, values, beliefs, principles, philosophy, attributes and characteristics. For example, here are four variants: Johnson and Johnson, Rabobank, Leo Burnett and UNICEF, which use very different terminology. It could be argued that both Johnson and Johnson and Leo Burnett are too long and convoluted, yet the ideas in the definition are particularly resonant in these organizations. The important criterion is that each seems to work. Generally it appears that the authenticity of and commitment to the brand idea is more important than the structure.

UNICEF

The UNICEF brand idea is contained within a brand book, which is given to all staff and suppliers. As well as containing the following definition of its brand, the book explains the relevance of the brand to the organization, provides explanations for each of the words and includes a question and answer section, which is based on the input of people from different departments.

The UNICEF brand

Following research and discussion we have developed a definition of the UNICEF brand that is relevant to us and helps us achieve our overall organizational objectives.

At the heart of what we exist to do is a core idea:

Working worldwide so that every child can reach their full potential

Often when we think about brands and make decisions about whether to buy something or donate to a cause, we think about three things. We think, is this organization effective? How is it different from other organizations? Do I feel good about this organization? To mirror this decision-making process, we have developed three further ideas that describe what we do functionally, comparatively and emotionally.

Functional (what we do, day in, day out)

UNICEF plays a leading role in the UK in changing attitudes and winning support for the fulfilment of the rights, including the needs, of every child.

Comparative (how we're different)

UNICEF is the global champion for children's rights which makes a lasting difference by working with communities and influencing governments.

Emotional (what motivates us)

United in making a difference for children.

The final element of the brand is the values we should convey. The following five words should help us define our attitudes and behaviour and also describe how we would like others to see us:

Effective
Cooperative
Challenging
Rights Based
Integrity

Leo Burnett

The Leo Burnett brand idea was defined long after the company's foundation, but its authenticity rests on the handed down wisdom of the founder, Leo Burnett.

Our Corporate Mission

The mission of the Leo Burnett Company is to create superior advertising. In Leo's words: 'Our primary function in life is to produce the best advertising in the world, bar none. This is to be advertising so interrupting, so daring, so fresh, so engaging, so believable and so well focused as to themes and ideas that, at one and the same time, it builds a quality reputation for the long haul as it produces sales for the immediate present.'

Operating Principles

Product: We recognise that the most important contribution we make to the success of our clients is Superior Advertising.

Clients: We will work with a select group of client who believe in advertising, whose businesses depend on Superior Advertising, who represent sizeable potential, who believe in partnership, and whose compensation policies and business ethics are compatible with our own.

People: We will employ only talented, idea-oriented people with high standards, who love advertising, demonstrate respect for other people, exhibit a sense of competitive pride, display an eagerness to excel and who put their client's interest before their own.

Environment: We will maintain a climate, in terms of working conditions, human relations, opportunities for growth, self expression, and monetary rewards, that will attract the best people and provide them with the most stimulating, rewarding and enjoyable career in the advertising business.

Organization: We will organize and staff to achieve our Superior Advertising Mission for every client, in every office; and, by going beyond that, to make a broad and positive contribution to the client's entire, on-going marketing effort.

Markets: We will operate only in markets where current or potential clients exist, or will exist, in a major way. Our offices, in any market where we do business, must be capable of delivering Superior Advertising.

New Business: We will plan and pursue an aggressive new business program, recognizing that new clients, and new assignments from existing clients, bring new challenges and opportunities, enhance our reputation, attract talented people, broaden our revenue base and contribute to the long-term health of the Agency. Since our primary responsibility is to current clients, new business should not take precedence over, nor get in the way of, those relationships.

Reputation: We will strive to be recognized as the best advertising agency in every market where we do business, based on our ability to produce Superior Advertising, to grow our client's business, to maintain enduring client relationships, to provide our people with the most stimulating and rewarding working environment and to conduct ourselves as responsible members of the communities where we do business.

Financial: We will be a privately-held company because that gives us the financial freedom to allocate our financial resources in the best interest of our clients and our people.

Integrity: We will operate, at all times, in an ethical and moral manner, as if Leo were looking over our shoulders.

Rabobank

Rabobank was founded some 100 years ago in the Netherlands as a cooperative to provide capital for farmers. The idea of partnership, which is an inherent element of cooperatives, survives to this day. Within the retail arm of the bank, each of the 425 branches has a manager and a small advisory board, which is chosen by the members (any customer, who is committed to the cooperative principles of the bank, can become a member). The customer boards come together yearly and every few months members of the boards meet with the management board in Utrecht. Any significant decision, such as a merger, has to involve the board members. To make this structure workable requires effective communication and the sharing of the organizational vision. The vision is presented within the Rabobank Group Ambition Statement, which in its terminology demonstrates the close relationship between customers and the bank. Following a statement about 'what we want to be', the Ambition Statement cites the following purpose and values:

Core Purpose

We, the staff and management of the Rabobank Group have, as both point of departure and primary goal the best interests of our customers. We aim to add value by:

- providing those financial services considered best and most appropriate by our customers;
- ensuring continuity in the services provided with a view to the long term interests of the client;
- commitment to our clients and their concerns and issues so that we can contribute to achieving their ambitions.

Core Values

We believe it is important that clients immediately recognise and personally experience the following values in all our activities:

- integrity: we act according to our stated aims;
- respect: we will interact with clients so that they experience our respect for them;
- expertise: we must be able to fulfil every promise we make.

Our Credo

We believe our first responsibility is to the doctors, nurses and patients,
to mothers and fathers and all others who use our products and services.
In meeting their needs everything we do must be of high quality.
We must constantly strive to reduce our costs
in order to maintain reasonable prices.
Customers' orders must be serviced promptly and accurately.
Our suppliers and distributors must have an opportunity
to make a fair profit.

We are responsible to our employees,
the men and women who work with us throughout the world.
Everyone must be considered as an individual.
We must respect their dignity and recognize their merit.
They must have a sense of security in their jobs.
Compensation must be fair and adequate,
and working conditions clean, orderly and safe.
We must be mindful of ways to help our employees fulfill
their family responsibilities.
Employees must feel free to make suggestions and complaints.
There must be equal opportunity for employment, development
and advancement for those qualified.
We must provide competent management,
and their actions must be just and ethical.

We are responsible to the communities in which we live and work
and to the world community as well.
We must be good citizens — support good works and charities
and bear our fair share of taxes.
We must encourage civic improvements and better health and education.
We must maintain in good order
the property we are privileged to use,
protecting the environment and natural resources.

Our final responsibility is to our stockholders.
Business must make a sound profit.
We must experiment with new ideas.
Research must be carried on, innovative programs developed
and mistakes paid for.
New equipment must be purchased, new facilities provided
and new products launched.
Reserves must be created to provide for adverse times.
When we operate according to these principles,
the stockholders should realize a fair return.

Johnson & Johnson

Figure 5.2 Johnson & Johnson credo

Structuring the brand idea

If an organization is starting afresh with defining a brand, or is reviewing its current articulation, my recommendation would be to use the UNICEF structure outlined above. This is because the structure is simple and it reflects the core characteristics of a brand. Here there is an overarching idea and then three supporting ideas plus a set of values:

- Core idea: the phrase tries to define the essence of the organization in as concise a way as possible. If an employee has to define the organizational brand to someone at a dinner party in one sentence this ought to be it.
- Functional idea: brands should always be a mixture of the functional and emotional. With strong brands such as Apple or Nike, there is both a functional product performance and an emotional bond. This sentence should therefore describe what the organization does in a descriptive way.
- Emotional idea: this ought to be the key motivator to people inside the company; the something that makes people skip up the stairs in the morning.
- Comparative idea: people choose to work for a company and engage with its purpose because it is different from other organizations. This idea should position the brand in people's minds in relation to other brands.
- Values: these articulate the most important beliefs of the organization.

Working with this structure, the creative group should try to deliver a brand articulation that is:

- memorable;
- true;
- all-encompassing;
- reinforcing;
- aspirational;
- differentiating.

Some of these words may sound contradictory and in themselves they are, but the key to success is that the totality of the brand definition meets these requirements:

- *Memorable*: one of the main failings of brand definitions is that they are overly complex. This is often a result of communications departments and brand consultancies working together to define a brand. As it is an area of particular interest to these individuals, they construct an idea that works for them. It is an exercise in intellectual insularity. However, pity the engineer who has to work out how to use the brand or the finance manager who has to decide which particular part of the brand description is relevant. Having worked with employees in using a brand, it is instructional to realize that it is only the obvious and memorable that really gets used. The rest is ignored. This also applies to the number of value words that the group defines. Employees will not use 12 or 15 words. They can understand and remember 6 words – although the fewer the better.
- *True*: put people together in a group and there is a danger that they will begin to develop group think traits – where the unity of the group becomes the dominant ideal. This can lead to wishful thinking and long-winded phrases that emanate from conversations, such as 'what we're really about is…and…and…and.' All the time the group should be trying to focus on what is true of the organization.
- *All-encompassing*: the definition should work for all parts of the organization and all levels of the hierarchy.
- *Reinforcing*: this is related to the idea of truth. Most organizations have things that are fundamental to their success. The brand should make those success factors explicit. Thus if creativity – as it is at Leo Burnett – is the bedrock of the organization, the brand statement should emphasize this.
- *Aspirational*: although wishful thinking should not be encouraged, the brand idea should propel the organization forwards to meet its goals. There should be an element of aspiration; of stretching people; of creating organizational tension.
- *Differentiating*: this should happen naturally if the group adheres to the above principles. There is little point in differentiating the organization for the sake of it. Remember these words and

phrases are for internal consumption. They are not advertising slogans. The process of differentiation will happen as a result of commitment and sincerity. For example, the US retailer, Nordstrom provides exceptional service to its customers, yet its brand definition words are those of a thousand other companies: service, quality, value, choice. It is the meaning these words have for Nordstrom that is particularly important.

Words, words, words [5]

There can be no reference source for the best brand words, but it is possible to match and test the ideas generated against the guidelines above. This helps to ensure that the words are true to the organization. To ensure that the words also motivate people we need to be sure that they tap into people's higher needs. If they do not, it will become apparent during the embedding stage – some ideas will simply be overlooked. However, rather than uncovering the problem later on it is better to try to evaluate the words at the front end of the process. To define the motivational impact of the words we need a tool. In a broad sense one can use Maslow's hierarchy of needs to check that the words do link in with feelings of esteem and self-actualization. Yet, there is another test, adapted from leadership training, which can help to determine the strength of the words.

The philosopher, Peter Koestenbaum, has identified that the best leaders operate in four dimensions: vision, reality, ethics and courage.[6] He argues that these four ways of thinking and acting, define long-term success. As these dimensions are concerned with the way people behave, they work equally well with brands:

- Visionary brands have a clear and precise sense of the future and have the knowledge and sensitivity to adapt to the needs of customers and other audiences.
- Reality is related to the idea of truth in the definition guidelines in the previous section and balances out the visionary. For just as a brand must understand the future it also needs to understand its limitations.

- Ethics denotes the fact that a brand needs to be principled; it needs to provide meaning to people and to encourage them to work together. This is particularly important in organizations, which bring together people from different competencies to work as a team.
- Courage is concerned with advocating and standing for something; it is about the willingness to take risks, to persuade others, and to be accountable for decisions.

Often brands operate in only one or two of these dimensions but just as Koestenbaum would argue that leaders need to possess all four, so do brands. This is what makes a brand distinctive and gives it a point of view that will bond some to it and frighten away others. Bland brands that do not possess courage or vision will only attract people by default. The distinctive and courageous brands that have been discussed in this book, such as Patagonia and Nike, attract people who share their values. To see how this works, relate the idea back to individuals. We admire people such as Mahatma Gandhi and Nelson Mandela because they operate in these four dimensions. If Mandela lacked a sense of reality, we'd say he was a dreamer. If Gandhi had no real vision people would not have followed him. Equally, if we saw that Patagonia was an unethical brand, it would be a less attractive company to work for.

Although Koestenbaum would argue for the presence of all four dimensions he would also advocate the primacy of courage. Courage is the hardest virtue to attain and maintain. It is always under threat because there are often easier choices that do not involve discomfort. It requires us to step out from what others do and confront the problem of free will. It requires us to choose. This is not a call to recklessness or indeed obstinacy. In a business context, it is about using knowledge to make the right decisions. It is Nike's decision to challenge the IOC, Greenpeace's to confront the GM industry and Patagonia's commitment to environmentalism. It is not about Coca-Cola's decision to relaunch a new version of Coke (courage without sensitivity or recklessness depending on your point of view) or Microsoft's confrontation with the US Government (obstinacy). As Koestenbaum says: 'But no significant decision – personal or organizational – has ever been undertaken without being attended by an existential crisis or without a commitment to wade through anxiety, uncertainty and guilt.'[7]

If a brand's values are going to challenge both managers and employees they need to stimulate people to be courageous. It is a further argument for a participative approach. It is not possible to stimulate courage in the organization if people feel they are unable or unwilling to take the difficult decisions and to act courageously. When people are free to choose and encouraged to make choices that support the brand then a sense of dynamism and power can emerge. Employees can begin to feel that they can change the world and fulfil their potential.

Just look again at the way Patagonia talks about its brand and you can see Koestenbaum's dimensions underlying it:

Patagonia: our purpose: (where we mean to take the company). *To use business to inspire and implement solutions to the environmental crisis.*

Our Core Values: (the characteristics that define the company).
Quality: Pursuit of ever-greater quality in everything we do.
Integrity: Relationships built on integrity and respect.
Environmentalism: Serve as a catalyst for personal and corporate action.
Not bound by convention: Our success – and much of the fun – lies in developing innovative ways to do things.

The problem with words

In articulating the brand idea the difficulty is producing words that meet the criteria set out above, motivate people, stir the imagination and have a reasonable constancy of meaning. Yet, as Wittgenstein observed, there is a problem with constancy of meaning. Our understanding of the words used to describe things or concepts varies over time and in tune with our own experience and cultural references. It is cubist in the sense that, as with painting, there can be many perspectives of the same thing. Rather than the certainty of classical painting, cubism suggests uncertainty and doubt: 'solid apprehensible reality seems to give way to a world of shifting relationships.' It is for the viewer or reader to make their own judgements. Words can pose questions as well as suggest answers. The semiotician and writer, Umberto Eco, brings this to life with his story of Marco Polo.[8] When Marco Polo visited Java, he was confronted by a rhinoceros – an animal he had never seen before. Rather than thinking this might be a new species, he used his existing frame of reference to categorize the animal. He concluded it must be a Unicorn – which was the only animal he knew of with a single horn protruding from its head. In describing the encounter, his sense of disappointment that the sensual horse with horn was rather a low-slung, armour-plated beast with a tongue made up of 'very long spines', is palpable. Thus to Polo and those that came into contact with him, the idea of a unicorn changed. Constancy is thus elusive. As Chomsky says: 'Terms are defined within a particular context and this context changes as people construct different empirical hypotheses. The terms then take on a different meaning.'[9]

There are two implications here. The first is the words used need to be precise and then carefully explained. One needs to employ a Socratic process of interrogation. If someone in the group working on the brand definition suggests that one of the key values is innovation, then:

- the members of the group should determine what the word 'innovation' really means for them;
- they should then ask, 'are we always innovative in this way?'
- if the answer is 'yes', innovation could be a reinforcing word – but only if the group feels it is an important aspect of the organization. If the answer is 'no, not always', the instances of non-innovation need to be discussed. This will determine whether innovation is something the organization does in pockets, but not overall or if the word is inappropriate. In the case of the latter, alternative words might be considered, such as 'creative', 'inventive' or 'ingenious' and the same process repeated. Often the right word appears through a process of negation – by defining what the organization is not or by relating it to competitors. People will say 'innovation is what company A is really good at and company B is very scientific and inventive, but what we are is creative';
- once the words have been agreed by the group, both the individual and the collective meanings need to be checked against the six criteria words above and against Koestenbaum's dimensions.

The second implication is that the group needs to recognize that both the words and the contexts will change. Brand ideas are designed for the long term but they are not impervious to evolution. For example, Johnson & Johnson, keeps its brand relevant, by continuously researching the idea of the credo with employees and then asking different groups within the company to challenge it every couple of years and to refine it, if necessary. Thus the essence of the Credo remains valid, but the nuances of meaning have changed gradually since it was first penned in the 1920s. Similarly Volvo uses a set of informal guidelines to articulate its philosophy. The informality is seen as important because it allows the philosophy to evolve as conditions change.

What should come out of the brand group discussion is a set of words that are robust in the sense that the group has challenged itself to generate powerful ideas and a set of contexts. The words will set a specific direction. The contexts will provide the necessary indicators of meaning. The real difficulty with generating brand words is that the lexicon is relatively small. For this reason, such words as 'innovative', 'integrity' and 'professional' are often repeated[10]. Sometimes organizations feel that using these words demonstrates a lack of insight. Surely, they argue, our organization is fundamentally different from our competitors and yet we end up defining ourselves in the same way. The response to this is that the ideal should be the selection of words that are as specific as possible. If an organization can find words that clearly set it apart, so much the better. For example, at Icon Medialab, alongside such words as 'professional' and 'passionate', 'inspired' and 'inspiring' are two words that are rare in the vocabulary of brands: 'kick-ass' and 'iconoclastic'. These two words define the challenging, questioning and assertive attitude of the company. They encourage the organization to do things differently and to take risks.

However, rather than focusing overtly on distinctive words, the goal should be to uncover what is in the organization. Truth is more important than linguistic inventiveness. In any case, the point of difference will come through from the context. For example, many organizations use the word 'professional' in their brand definitions. Yet it will not mean exactly the same thing in a law firm and a government department. There will be some degree of constancy, such as always providing a prompt service, being thorough and delivering comprehensive documentation. Then there will be organization-specific inferences. For the law firm it might be connected to quality of research and for the government department it might link to proactive advice to ministers. These ideas will be derived from an expectation of what is important to succeed as an organization and from the experience of past success. Thus the law firm might conclude that the reason it wins work is because it conveys a professional image. It might argue that part of acting professionally is being well informed through high quality research. Thus for this company, professionalism might be defined as:

> Always being well informed and responding to client requests promptly and efficiently. Professionalism means we always document everything we do thoroughly. It means setting ourselves high standards and then challenging ourselves and each other to exceed them. It means focusing on our clients.

Thus 'professionalism' starts to mean something more specific. The definition does not aim to be proscriptive. It does not say you must do this and mustn't do that, but rather it indicates the layers of intended meaning. Once the brand becomes embedded and ideas of how to use 'professional' are implemented throughout the organization the meaning will then acquire greater breadth and depth.

Checking the words

Once the initial brand definition has been agreed, there should be a final check on the words. The creative group should have been representative of the organization, but perhaps certain departments or overseas offices have not been fully involved in the process. This point has particularly significant connotations, because vision and value words can have different meanings across the world. The nature of business in different countries also creates different emphases. For example, research into the most important values for American and Swedish business people revealed that for Americans, 'honesty' is the most important value. Yet for the Swedish, the word did not even rate a mention. The litigiousness of the United States makes the notion of honesty a key issue but for Swedes the idea is implicit in business practice and, indeed, society. Thus you don't need to state honesty overtly because there is an assumption that people will do the right thing without being told to do so. These differences are highlighted by Charles Hampden-Turner and Fons Trompenaars,[11] who have researched the cultural differences between societies that are universalist (believe in rules, codes, laws and generalizations) and particularist (believe in exceptions, circumstances and relations). Countries such as Norway and Switzerland are particularly universalist and Russia and Yugoslavia are more particularist. The more universalist the culture, the greater the tendency to abide by rules and codes. For a nationally focused organization, these cultural variances are not important, but for any regional or global organization these differences are vital. It indicates the importance of involving overseas offices in deciding on the words to be used and subsequently it suggests that the meaning of the words needs to include people's different cultural assumptions.

The most effective way to determine the validity of the chosen words is to share them with the organization. For example, when VSO undertook its brand programme it used the creative group to define the words and then it issued them electronically and in paper format to its employees who work in 60 different countries. To reiterate the importance of the process, the text presented the definition of the brand and the rationale behind it. It then detailed a clear timetable and the potential benefits of articulating the brand. It then posed three questions:

- Does this proposal capture the essence of VSO?
- Is this brand meaningful for me?
- What impact would this have on my work?

Some employees returned individual responses, while others got together in groups and discussed the implications of the words. They sought out nuances that the creative group had never considered and they made suggestions as to improving the phrases and words. The important thing was that, in deconstructing the brand idea, they began the process of uncovering its meaning for themselves. The responses were considerable but the brand group went through all of them and reconsidered the brand definition in the light of the different inputs. As a result, the brand and the meanings attributed to the words evolved. The text acquired subtleties that had not been there before. Once the words were agreed, the brand was presented to the trustees and the management group for approval.

An alternative to this approach is to create an e-mail forum or a chat room about the brand. The advantage of this approach is the ongoing interaction. For example, the first round of the forum, might outline the suggested values and invite people to pass judgement in line with the three questions above. People not only have the opportunity to put forward their own ideas, but they can also pass comment on the thoughts of others. After a specified amount of time, which can be anything from a few hours to a few days, the moderator provides a summary and poses any further clarification questions. Following any final comments, the round is closed off and the second round commences. This might look at the functional, comparative and emotional statements. Again the process is repeated. Finally, the core idea is scrutinized. Once all the comments are received, the moderator provides a final report and asks everyone to confirm the accuracy of the input.

Summary

This chapter has been about the process of brand definition but it recognizes that definition can also be part of the process of embedding the brand. Some organizations and consultancies adopt a more top-down approach to definition, believing it to be something that communication experts should undertake and then disseminate. From experience I would disagree. The more participative the definition process, the greater the chance that people will feel like the brand is their own. This, in turn, helps generate understanding and commitment. If the communication department tries to impose an idea then the process of building support will be harder and the tendency to see the brand as something to do with logo creation or marketing programmes, stronger. The difficulty for some organizations is that the process is time consuming. However, the benefits of front end buy in from employees outweighs the negatives. It is potentially more time consuming to rush the front end and then have to work doubly hard at the embedding process.

Notes

1 Van Riel, CBM (1995) *Principles of Corporate Communication*, Prentice-Hall, Englewood Cliffs, p 50.
2 Hatch, Mary Jo and Schultz, Majken (1997) Relations between organizational culture, identity and image, *European Journal of Marketing*, **31** (5/6), p 362.
3 Research by MORI indicates that one in five people in organizations in Britain can be classified as saboteurs.
4 Van Rekom J, paper presented at First Corporate Identity Symposium, Strathclyde University, 1994.
5 *Hamlet* – Hamlet to Polonius, Act II, Scene II.
6 See www.pib.net for further details.
7 Labarre, Polly, interview with Peter Koestenbaum, Fast Company, March 2000, p 230.
8 Eco, Umberto (1999) *Kant and the Platypus: Essays on language and cognition*, Secker & Warburg, London, pp 57–58.
9 Chomsky, Noam (1998) *On Language*, The New Press, New York, p 171.
10 ORC International Research (2000) found that 38 per cent of global businesses have 'customer service/care/satisfaction' in their brand statements (49 per cent in the United States), while 25 per cent have 'quality' and 23 per cent 'innovation'.
11 Hampden-Turner, Charles and Trompenaars, Fons (2000) *Building Cross-Cultural Competence*, John Wiley & Sons, Chichester.

Bringing **the brand to life**

Many organizations have well-constructed brand statements. Some even have well-produced booklets or brochures about their brands. Few move beyond the presentation to deliver the substance. It seems it's easier to talk about the brand than to live it. Living the brand requires commitment and sincerity and that means it has to permeate the whole organization. Whoever the original brand owner is – whether it is the CEO, the board, the marketing department or human resources – they need to share the idea of the brand with the organization. While the originator should set a strong example and might steer the overall direction, employees need to feel it is their brand, that they can understand it in their own terms and contribute to its development. This requires some humility. The communications director might like everyone to know who was really behind the latest creation but there is greater benefit in getting other departments involved as quickly as possible and in communications moving to an influential, but not overtly dominant role.

If the articulation process has been participative then the organization will already know about the brand and understand its potential value. However, if the organization already has a long-established brand definition and is now seeking to make it more effective then the methodology needs to be amended. Prior to the embedding, management will need to persuade the organization of the value of taking branding seriously – this will require presentations and discussion fora where the nature and impact of the brand can be explored. Once the purpose of branding is better understood, there are a series of mechanisms that can begin the process of establishing the brand in people's day to day lives. These include:

- brand books, games, plays and videos;
- brand champions;
- brand workshops;
- events.

Brand books, games and videos

The purpose of a brand book is to present the brand and its context. This should be an opportunity to reinforce the value of the brand, its relationship to other activities and strategies in the organization and the anticipated benefits. Both the look and the language of the book need to be carefully considered. It will often be the first clear presentation of what the brand stands for and as such it will send a signal to all employees. Unless the brand idea steers the design of the book the process can founder here. Thus if one of the brand values is inspiring, then the book itself should reflect that idea. Equally if straightforward is a value, the presentation should not obfuscate – rather it should concentrate on delivering a clear message.

The text should also adopt an 'insider' tone. Although the copy should be well crafted, employing a copywriter has dangers. The document should be seen as a message from one employee to another: our brand, not a consultant's. Thus the language should be positive, supportive, engaging and persuasive, but it should not indulge in hyperbole. This is a fine line to tread and not easily achievable, but if you look at a selection of brand books you can see the difference between sincerity and superficiality. The sincere output does not over-claim; it suggests rather than sells. It should provide evidence for its ideas and show the context by demonstrating examples. In the case of UNICEF the contexts were provided by recording the core ideas of the brand group rather than writing the text independently.

While defining what should be in the brand book, there are also some things that should not be included. This is a guide to attitudes and behaviour, not a rulebook. Therefore, there should be no instructions or diktats. Nor is it a visual identity manual or guide to communications. If the brand book is for everyone from technicians to receptionists then there is little point in providing detailed instructions on the use of the logo or typography. It also tends to encourage people to think again that brands are about logos, not about behaviour.

The final point about the book is that it should have the capacity to be updated. At its simplest this suggests the inclusion of some form of insert but if the book is to be published on the company intranet this may afford a more practical and effective mechanism. The updating element is partly connected to the opportunity to allow the words themselves to evolve but, more importantly, it provides the means of sharing best practice and keeping the brand in people's minds. Just as when a brand is communicated to external audiences it has to fight for mindshare, so it has to internally. As examples of effective brand usage arise from within the organization, whether they be from finance or operations or human resources, they should be posted and advertised on the intranet. Discussion groups can also be set up to enable people from all over the organization to join in debates about the brand and its usage. All of this can only be sustained if there is a genuine interest in the brand and employees can see that it has real and practical benefits.

As the updatability argument indicates, there are limitations with a printed format but it is something that people can keep and to which they can refer. It should be usable, rather than read once and then consigned to a filing cabinet. Nonetheless the book itself should not be the only means of communicating the brand. There are opportunities to create posters, promotional items and internal newsletters. There is also the option of games, videos and even plays. The benefit of these items is their potential for engagement. Take games, for example. Books are instructive. They send a message to us, we absorb it momentarily, we may feel inspired and then mostly we forget what we have read. Thus a brand book can only be a reminder or reference source. In contrast a game has the potential for involvement and repetition. The value of repetition, when it is of our choosing, is that it shapes our minds. We absorb the message. For example, take a card game, such as Bridge. It is a complex game, especially for the beginner, because of the protocols that surround the bidding process and the need for a good memory. You could read a book, entitled something like *How to Win at Bridge*, or you could play the game 20 times. If you do the latter you begin to understand how the game works, how your opponents think, how to gamble and how to win. You gain an insight into competitiveness, risk, creativity and probably disappointment. You learn by osmosis. Now take a brand idea and convert it into a game. It could be a quiz type game or a quest or a challenge. The important thing is that underlying the outward façade of the game are the vision and values. Employees learn about the values, not by being told them, but by experiencing them in an environment that gives the illusion of reality. The Web provides a perfect environment for doing this because it can create virtual worlds that mimic the working environment. For example, if an organization wants to encourage international cooperation, the sharing of knowledge and questioning, the game can be based around crossfunctional international teams that have to travel the globe in search of clues, which they have to solve. The teams can search out information by asking an oracle and they might receive emails suggesting alternative ways of looking at problems. To make it more sophisticated, artificial intelligence can be built into the game so that team unity and team knowledge determines the ease with which the group can progress. Games such as this enable us to learn about things in a safe context. It is a close parallel with how children learn: through roleplay, analysis, using their imagination and stretching their capabilities.

Brand champions

Trying to create support for a brand idea from the centre is an almost impossible task. Many far-flung offices, especially if they have acquired some cynicism, will ignore or perhaps even ridicule attempts to impose an idea. There is also the common feeling that business units and brand offices have their own culture, which is independent of whatever the corporate head office might like to suggest. The task here is not to undermine that localized culture but to add another layer to it so that people can still feel an affinity with perhaps cherished and long-held beliefs, *and* engage with a larger corporate purpose. This requires local representation in every key functional and geographic area, in the form of committed individuals who are willing to proselytize on behalf of the brand; people who have the respect of colleagues and believe in the power of branding. The role of these brand champions is to:

- communicate the brand idea to colleagues;
- encourage involvement;

- make recommendations to the centre on brand issues;
- set and measure targets;
- share best practice.

They should have the capability to run effective workshops and the confidence to promote the cause of the brand to others. The brand champions are vital disseminators and standard bearers. This helps to counter the danger of a loss of impetus: an issue that can easily arise if the originator of the programme leaves or is transferred. For this reason, there should also be a brand champion at Board level, so that senior managers appreciate that they too should set an example within their own departments.

Brand workshops

To generate active involvement with the brand and to create meaning, each team within the organization should undertake an initial brand workshop. To reinforce the point about consistency of communication, each team member should be asked to write a one-sentence description of what the core purpose of the organization is. If the organization engages in a complex activity it is often instructive to see how the variety of descriptions could easily confuse any potential recipient. VSO stressed this point in a sketch they produced for staff and which they subsequently transformed into a video. The video film shows a split screen with two individuals typing a letter to the same person. One is a fundraiser and the other a campaigner. Their messages are diametrically opposite. One is talking about needy people in Africa, whereas the other is writing about development education.

Once the initial one-liner exercise has been done, the brand champion should outline the purpose of the organization. This then leads naturally into a discussion about the brand and its meaning. The most useful thing to focus on at this point is the core idea and the values. These should guide the process. The workshop can be structured tightly or it can use brainstorming techniques. It can involve using images and words and the creation of scenarios – anything that helps people to imagine how the brand can unlock some of the things they do currently. At this first workshop, the goal should be to agree on a specific number of targets, based around current activities. The point of rooting this activity in the present is that it helps to generate rapid change and it focuses on things that are achievable. The number of targets also needs to be limited. Brainstorming can generate lots of good ideas but the subsequent weeding out should help to determine the real priorities. To avoid woolliness the wording of these recommendations should be as precise as possible, be tightly linked to the brand idea and be measurable. The last is important if the impact of the brand on activity is to be judged. I would also argue that the recommendations for each team be publicly displayed on the intranet and on notice boards, so that people can see the aims of others and to spot overlaps and areas of potential cooperation.

The workshop should not, of course, be a one-off event but the beginning of a series of workshops that relate the brand to organizational goals. As people become more familiar with the brand and what it means, the workshops can evolve in two ways. They can start to become more focused on the future; on longer term initiatives that might change significantly the way a specific team works. Secondly, they can become more focused: looking, for example, at the way a press team writes press releases or the finance team provides information to colleagues. The important thing is that the brand and what it stands for remain the guiding light.

Events

Events in themselves will not generate commitment to the brand – they can only help to embed it in support of some of the activities suggested above. The value of an event is that it can help to heighten interest in the brand and it provides the opportunity for the brand owner and champions to campaign on behalf of the brand. The most appropriate events are those that support subtly, by their nature, the idea of the brand. This is an opportunity for people to live the brand in a very active way. For example, if the brand is about discovery and challenge, then the event ought to incorporate activities that encourage this. It might involve a presentation on the topic and then a team-based project that involves people travelling around and uncovering new ideas and recording their interactions with people. The Dutch IT company Origin, (a merger of BSO and Philips) which has defined its values as: freedom, responsibility, integrity and orginality, organizes scientifically oriented expeditions to the four corners of the globe. These expeditions, which generate large numbers of applicants from within the organization and which have also appeared on Dutch television, are structured around the values and deliberately designed to promote them through active participation. Geerd Schlangen, ex-communications director of Origin, says: 'The expeditions are a mixture of adventure, teamwork and science – where we can try out new technologies. They're also a metaphor for the way people behave at Origin.'

Similarly, when SAS launched their new identity to staff in 1999, they brought people together to present the new visual identity and also to play a travel experience game involving multi functional teams that was designed to embed the brand idea, enable people to understand each other's perspectives and to extend the idea of friendship through sharing and participating.

Human resources

Apart from the communications group within an organization the other key proponents of the brand should be the human resources team. The brand should permeate the recruitment, rewards, training and development process. Each of these elements is important individually, but most important is that they all point in the same direction. There is little value in creating a brand-led human resources system that encourages a certain trait, if organizational rewards stimulate the opposite behaviour. This requires human resources personnel to think strategically; to relate their initiatives to the brand idea. This is an ideal, which HR managers would probably argue for, but the evidence suggests that the strategic orientation is often missing. Citing research from the Laborforce 2000 survey of 406 senior human resource executives, Jeffrey Pfeffer, notes that 'one out of every four HR departments says that *none* of their company's business strategies are a major responsibility of their department.'[1] One in five executives cite changes to benefit and compensation plans as their best decisions. The major barrier to developing more involving human resource practices is seen to be the cost of making changes. The problem for developing a more brand-focused human resources strategy is that there are implementation and ongoing costs in reworking recruitment procedures, developing new appraisal and reward systems and investing in electronic and actual learning material and support. Management wants to be reassured of the benefits of this upheaval yet prior to undertaking the change the likely benefits can only be informed guesses. As Matthew Bell of VSO says: 'The Chief Executive and senior management will not buy-in from the start. They will need to be persuaded – theoretically first, and then by the evidence of its impact (the brand programme) around the organization…The idea of a brand may seem irrelevant or opaque.'

To reduce the opacity it is important that measurement systems are put in place to evaluate the impact of human resource initiatives. For example, if there is a significant investment in training then the benefits of this in terms of increased knowledge, skills and productivity should be measured.

Recruitment

The brand process starts here with the very nature of recruitment advertising and literature. The people an organization employs and the degree to which their personal values match those of the brand are essential elements within the brand process. This, of course, is not a static process. People's values will change over time, as will the nature of the brand, and it is possible for them to get out of kilter. However, the better the match at the outset the greater the likelihood that the individual and the corporate values will adjust to meet each other's needs. Thus the nature of the brand needs to be clearly communicated through all recruitment messages. These interactions should be carefully structured so that an accurate picture of the values is conveyed. The reality is often different. Look at any business or current affairs publication and you will see a plethora of distinctive advertisements that convey imagery far removed from the organizational identity. Partly this seems to do with wishful thinking and partly with a desire to be different. An example of this was a research project I undertook for a client that was struggling to get the right sort of applicants. It became clear that the tone of the recruitment advertising was clearly misplaced. It not only misrepresented the organization by making exaggerated claims but it was a turn off to the would-be applicants. As a result the organization changed the tone of its language and also its choice of media.

Once the organization receives responses to its recruitment communication, the brand can also determine which people to interview. This is hard to achieve if one is relying on CVs, but an application form can be so structured as to help unearth the likely values match. To take an extreme example, if one wanted to work for Greenpeace, which adopts a confrontational stance on environmental action, then you probably have to identify quite closely with the organization's goals and its beliefs. This suggests that a Greenpeace application form should probe an individual's ideals and willingness to take direct action in support of them. Once organizations reach the interview stage many employ scoring mechanisms or structured interview guides. These, too, can incorporate aspects that help to ascertain the closeness of the match between individuals and the organization. The only concern in this process is that generating too many clones can be dangerous and produce groupthink. The Dutch IT company, Pink Elephant, found that it was so successful at recruiting like-minded individuals that it stopped questioning itself and the way it did things. It developed a comfortable collegiate atmosphere which people enjoyed but was ultimately detrimental to the brand. Now it consciously focuses on recruiting some mavericks – people who sit outside the recruitment norm of the organization.

Training

Once people are employed by the organization the training process should be so structured as to embed the values. This should start with the induction programme. As we saw with Scient and its SPARK programme, induction is a real opportunity to help build understanding about the brand and to align people to its principles. Outside of brainwashing, this indicates why people need a predisposition towards the brand in the first place. People can sometimes uncover suppressed aspects of their character on these occasions but it is likely that if they possess contradictory beliefs, the whole experience will be uncomfortable. The danger is that, in a desire to fit in, individuals will try to adapt their idea of self to the organizational norm. In the short term this may be achievable but it has the potential to create psychological damage. This is most notable in organizations that have highly explicit codes of behaviour, such as the Army, schools and religious institutions.

If the brand values are geared towards helping the organization achieve its overall objectives, the training process should focus on creating programmes that are defined by the values. For example, if creativity is a core value then people's creative abilities need to be nurtured. This is inevitably easier for some than others. People who have creative backgrounds step into the idea of creating collages or building scenarios or brainstorming new ideas easier than perhaps engineers. The key here is to try to focus the idea of creativity on what is relevant to people's backgrounds. If we think through the sort of creativity we want engineers to engage with, we can construct training accordingly. Perhaps we want engineers to question accepted ways of doing things and to seek inspiration from other business areas. We might construct a training programme that encourages people to adapt lessons learned from previous careers or hobbies to re-evaluate their established way of tackling issues. In their paper, 'Building an Innovation Factory', Andrew Hargadon and Robert Sutton,[2] cite how the product design consultancy IDEO encourages innovation. People are encouraged to use their backgrounds or interests, such as toys or cars, to create new ideas. Transferring knowledge from one area to another is a vital element and each office has 'tech boxes' in which interesting materials and products are stored. The curators of the 'tech boxes' keep the contents updated on the intranet so that people know where to look for specific inspiration.

To get people to realize their creativity you have to unleash them from the rational constraints of their everyday jobs. They have to think different, before they can act different. Gordon MacKenzie in his *Orbiting the Giant Hairball* provides an interesting example of this. He relates how he was asked to attend a regional sales meeting for Hallmark to inject some creativity into the proceedings. Having suffered soporific overheads of sales charts, he began his session by dimming the lights, lighting candles and asking people to close their eyes. He then clashed two cymbals together and asked people to imagine a flower floating inside their heads. The flower then made a transcendental journey through everyone's body before being released. As people opened their eyes MacKenzie asked them to tell him everything they hated about sales meetings. They filled six pages on the flipchart. Then he asked them to create a sales meeting structure that would be effective:

> The group exploded. The shell of their corporate reserve split open and a breathtaking flood of pent-up, common-sense, know-how transformed their arid, grey conference room into a cauldron of creativity. Eagerness, enthusiasm, optimism filled the air. Everyone threw ideas on the table with joyous abandon.[3]

Although generating creative thought seems to have been achieved in this instance, the far harder task, of course, is sustaining it. Building commitment and encouraging change will always be easier with those aspects of the brand and its values that are well established within the organization. The more aspirational the value the harder it is to maintain. It will require ongoing training and a conscious attempt to develop the organization and its methods in the relevant way.

One of the developments that is helping continuous training is the development of e-learning. This is the use of CD-ROMs and intranets to facilitate self-learning. This can take place either at people's work-stations, in a learning centre or in a corporate university (of which there are already 400 in the United States). At parts supplier Unipart, the company university is carried through into the 'faculty on the floor'. These are shop-floor learning centres where people can go to develop their skills through e-learning packages, which they can apply immediately to their jobs.

The value of the centres is then extended by their use for team meetings, problem-solving activities and quality circles. The benefits that Unipart and others receive from their commitment to e-learning are several. The standard of delivery is consistent, the costs are less than formalized classroom-based training, it is adaptable to people's needs in that a course can be used as a total learning experience, a pre-live-course, live module, or a post-course refresher, and it is time effective in that it can be used whenever people need it.

However, there are still some limitations with e-learning. It should not be seen as a substitute for classroom training, but rather as an additional channel. Classroom experience provides valuable one-to-one interaction that cannot be replicated online. Equally, some people within organizations do not have access to a computer. This is especially true for people who are mobile or do manual tasks. Although courses can be bought off the shelf, they can also be tailored to the needs of the organization and of the brand. The concept below provides a simple example of an e-learning module built around brand values. It is designed for a telecommunications organization and is meant to teach such ideas as client orientation, teamwork and environmentalism.

The module initially asks the participant to chose where they want to work within the organization (frame 1). In this variant, the choice is the shop (frame 2). In the shop, the participant can click any of the products and learn about the product details and customer benefits (frame 3). Now customers come into the shop and ask a question. They know that the company is environmentally responsible and they want to know if the company can dispose of a telephone answering machine. The participant doesn't know the answer, but he can seek advice from either the intranet, a colleague, or a telephone centre (frame 4). He chooses 'colleague'. She appears and gives advice on environmental policy (frame 5). The participant can now click on a box that provides an answer to the customer (frame 6). The customer is happy and so is the participant (frame 7). The participant now has to confirm what he has learned from the experience (frame 8). Finally, he gets feedback from the manager (frame 9).

Appraisals and rewards

The values should define the way appraisals are conducted. For example, values such as being collaborative, cooperative and unified indicate that appraisals should evaluate peoples' capacity

(1)
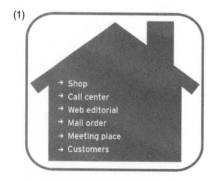

(2)

Figure 6.1 e-learning concept

and willingness to work with colleagues. Values such as being inspired, challenging and questioning would suggest the importance of peoples' ability to confront the status quo and to always seek better ways of doing things. The appraisal process then leads into the nature of rewards. Unless human resources are actively involved in the development of the brand, there is always the risk that an intellectually well-structured articulation is undermined because people are rewarded if they behave in a non-brand way. If the appraisal and reward system in an organization is strongly biased towards rewarding individual business performance, this reduces the likelihood of people working collaboratively. This may be appropriate if the value is individualism, but not very conducive if it is partnership. Then it would be more effective to reward individual and team based behaviour. At IDEO, where collaboration is seen as key to the innovation process, people are rewarded in part by the review each person gets from colleagues. In their book *Paying for Contribution* (Kogan Page, 1999), Michael Armstrong and Duncan Brown note that organizations are increasingly moving away from a narrow view of performance-related pay to a more inclusive approach that encompasses an individual's competence and contribution and rewards individual, team and organizational performance. This is an encouraging sign, which suggests that there is an increased likelihood of the use of reward structures that can be aligned in support of corporate values.

Recruitment, training, appraisals and rewards

These elements have been described individually, but they need to be seen as a whole. The human resources strategy from beginning to end needs to be steered by the brand idea. This ensures that the right people are hired in the first place, that they are treated well, receive appropriate training and are rewarded effectively. If any individual element is out of line it will upset the continuity of the whole. For example, at the booksellers Waterstones, the brand is built around the idea of a bookshop for book lovers. When the company was started in 1982 it had certain key characteristics: it offered a wide range, it had knowledgeable staff who shared the customer's passion for books and it provided an ambience similar to that of a traditional library. Given these characteristics, which are still maintained, it is perhaps not surprising that 75 per cent of the booksellers are graduates and in a staff survey 98 per cent said that reading was a passion or a consuming passion. Consequently, attracting and nurturing the right people is at the heart of the brand. The appeal for employees is in part their opportunity for participation. Employees write book reviews for Waterstone publications and provide recommendations to customers, and each manager orders his or her own stock and they deliver service in their own way. Recognizing that good booksellers do not necessarily make good managers, nor perhaps desire to be them, the company also evolved a rewards structure that enables people to maintain their position while enjoying salary levels commensurate with promoted staff.

Internal communications

Internal communication is important in two respects. First, it can convey the benefits of the brand idea and encourage involvement. This requires the active dissemination of good practice and the sharing of results. Second, external communication campaigns (assuming they are true to the brand) should be marketed internally. The first point is important, because there is always a temptation to see brands as something ephemeral – the realm of the marketing department, not the whole organization. Therefore, all the mechanisms available to the organization – direct contact, intranet, briefings, research and internal publications – need to keep reiterating the importance of the brand to overall performance. This process is helped if research is used to evaluate the impact of the brand on organizational awareness, sales, profits, performance figures and rankings. Qualitative research and anecdotes also add to the brand mythology, especially if the stories are nurtured within the organization, but some parts of the organization are more likely to be persuaded by hard figures – especially those that relate to the bottom line. The company intranet can be particularly valuable to the process of sustaining interest in the brand. The opportunity to build online communities enables the brand to become a focus for discussion, rather than something people just hear about.

When it comes to the internal marketing of external campaigns, the degree of commitment varies. At its best, companies treat employees as a key audience. They involve them in the research process and structure the campaign idea with employees consciously in mind. This helps to ensure that advertising or direct marketing campaigns can be easily supported by employees who not only understand the content but are, to a degree, involved in the message. This is particularly notable when the external campaign itself stretches employee behaviour towards meeting corporate goals. This is always a delicate balance: push it too far and people can feel disassociated from the idea. However, as was observed in the New York Port Authority case, the perceived external image of the organization among employees can be a significant determinant of attitudes and behaviour. It can generate a sense of pride or a renewed commitment to professionalism or innovation or whatever the central message of the campaign is. It can enhance people's sense of self-esteem and actualization. Of course, the opposite also applies. When there is negative press commentary about an organization, it may have an external impact on consumer behaviour or the desirability of working for a particular company, but it can also undermine employees' sense of esteem and confidence. Rather than their peers commending their choice of career, a potential sense of condemnation emerges. This can be particularly painful if the source of criticism runs counter to individual beliefs. For example, Nike has been criticized for the labour conditions in some of the factories that produce its products in the Far East. The impact of this was particularly profound on employees, many of whom had joined the company because it seemed to represent a different idea of business: an anti-establishment organization that was focused on sport, not on bottom lines – the Robin Hood of corporate America. Yet the company seemed to be acting like a robber baron. Nelson Farris of Nike says:

> One of the biggest mistakes we made was to think we don't own the factories, so that's their problem. That's when we recognised we were more powerful than we realised and as a consequence, people expected more of us. Employees were embarrassed and disenchanted and confused. The media had sweatshops and child labour in every sentence. They thought we were covering up, which we weren't...Part of our culture is to do the right thing and we've been pretty good at it. But the fact we did not get in front of the child labour issue did cause us grief.

As the Nike example suggests, it is not possible to control communications. Positive and negative messages will appear. The task from a branding point of view is to ensure the active engagement of employees in the communication of positive messages and the accurate stating of the issues when the message is negative. There is a belief among many organizations that they do not get a fair hearing from the media. This is a particular claim of politicians, who seem to view the media as deliberately misrepresenting their ideas. Large businesses also often seem to feel similarly threatened. Mostly their response is to think they should improve their communications: spend more on advertising, develop better PR programmes, create a more effective Web site. Generally this is misplaced. Organizations tend to get a hard time from the media because they underperform: they fail to listen to customers, they don't support their employees, they don't act in a socially responsible way or they don't live up to their promises. This is Professor Stephen Greyser commenting on Exxon and the late 1980s ecological disaster of the oil spill in Alaska:

> In June 1994, headlines proclaimed, 'Jury finds Exxon acted recklessly in Valdez oil spill'. This was another chapter, five years after the start, of a story born in disaster in Alaska's Prince William Sound...nurtured in what I consider misconceived apologetic Exxon communications to soften the blow and refurbish its image...and still after five years punctuated by negative headlines! The problem? Not communications... but substance. It is Exxon's behaviour that is being judged by the public to have fallen short.[4]

Even when corporate behaviour is positive or an advertising campaign is designed to convey a particular message about the organization it can be difficult to garner support from employees. Most often this is because they have not been seriously considered as an audience to communicate with. Sometimes communication directors and their advertising agencies only show their campaigns after they have been created, as a way of informing employees. On other occasions even this is overlooked. There was a particularly noteworthy campaign in the United Kingdom, for retailer J Sainsbury, which featured a strident John Cleese conveying the idea that the staff were slow and stupid. It would be surprising if this had involved the active engagement of staff. In fact it created an uproar among the employees and the campaign was stopped and the advertising agency fired. It did few favours for anyone involved, including Cleese. The conclusion ought to be that employees, should be treated as the equals of consumers in the development of external campaigns.

Working with brand communications

Most staff will probably not be involved in developing marketing communications but a number of people will have responsibilities for briefing and overseeing external messages. In smaller organizations this may be the province of a single individual but in larger organizations there can be literally hundreds of people producing brochures, leaflets, Web sites, public relations campaigns and advertising. While all these forms of communication need not be slavishly the same, they ought to reflect the overall organizational brand. In part this can be achieved through policing mechanisms but a more effective means is by working with these communicators so that they understand the implications for the brand in external communications. This can have a dual impact again. It undoubtedly has an effect on the attitudes of external audiences, but these communications are an important signalling device to other employees. If a new brand articulation has been agreed by the organization, high-profile external campaigns or visual identities will become more significant as indicators of organizational intent.

As with the workshops for staff, discussed earlier in this chapter, there should also be specific workshops for communicators. These can afford to be more sophisticated and detailed, as these communication professionals will need to be able to address ongoing and potentially complicated brand issues and be able to brief and work effectively with external agencies. Using stimuli material to provoke debate, some or all of the following issues might be addressed:

- branding principles and terminology;
- the articulation of the organizational brand: extending from the internal vision and values into the external personality and positioning;
- the brand structure;

- implications for brand innovation and extension;
- approaches to co-branding and endorsing third-party activities;
- branding on the Internet;
- briefing agencies and consultancies.

Vision, values, personality and positioning

The chart overleaf shows the various aspects of a brand. In the internal sphere are the vision and values (or whatever the agreed terminology). These give a sense of the future and define the beliefs of the organization. They are connected to a way of thinking and behaving. However, although they are primarily internal, they impact on the way the organization presents itself externally.

They should form part of the briefing process for external communications and they should form part of the template against which identities and communications are judged. In addition to vision and values, the brand should also be defined in terms of its personality and positioning. The values indicate what people believe, but personality defines how the organization conveys itself. Obviously these two concepts should not be divorced from each other. Although it can be dangerous to use the analogy of individual personalities, it is useful to try to discuss the organization in the same way we might talk about a person. Thus, for example, we might determine that the brand's personality is connected to ideas of friendliness, approachability, wit and ambition. The purpose of defining a positioning is that every brand has to compete for a consumer's mind space and therefore it is valuable to position the brand relative to its key competitors from a consumer perspective.

Brand structure

This area can be enormously complicated but it involves trying to think through how to present the brand to external audiences. This involves determining how the organization's name is related to geographic areas, business units, sub-brands, product names and service or channel descriptors. At one extreme the Virgin model can be adopted where the Virgin brand name and logo is attached to all

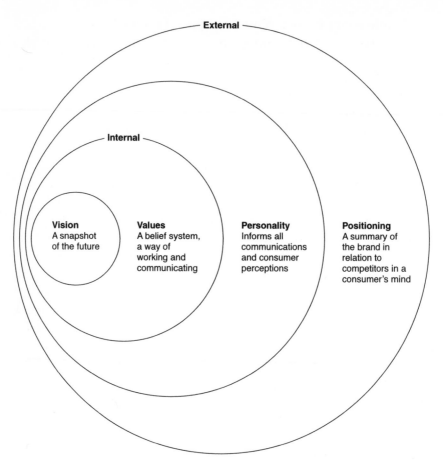

Figure 6.2 The onion

presentations of the brand. At the other end is the Procter & Gamble (P & G) model, where the company's products, such as Pampers, Ariel and Pringles are not associated with the parent company. However, most companies are situated somewhere in between linking some products more overtly to the parent name than others. The overall modular approach depends on the organizational goals. The value of the Virgin model is the economies of communication that are achieved and the inbuilt brand expectation with which consumers approach a new product launch. The advantage of the P & G system is that it is possible to segment audiences and therefore build category share without confusing the customer. The most common mistake in developing brand structures is to assume that they have to mirror organizational structures. They do not. Brand structures should be focused around how consumers or other audiences see the brand, not how management positions units on an organizational chart. Nor should people confuse brands with delivery channels or products. Sometimes organizations go to great lengths to create structures that convey the subtleties of what they do. Thus, as well as the parent brand, we also get a variety of geographic descriptors (Europe, Americas, Asia) and channel descriptors (.com, wireless, events, retail). This may be appropriate if they are simply descriptors, but sometimes these words are tagged onto the parent brand. This can be important to managers, but probably consumers just see the parent.

The degree to which products and brands are associated with the parent, depends largely on the transference of value. The value the parent confers on its sub brands and products and the flow backwards should help determine how to present the relationships within the organization. To help communicators address this problem of structure, Phil Rushton of Icon Medialab has developed a brand innovator's decision tree. The example below shows how someone can judge the branding approach for a new business concept within an overall group.

Co-branding and endorsing

Often when brands are presented they are connected to other brands. This is becoming increasingly prevalent because of the networked nature of many businesses. However, simply putting two or more logos together is a simplistic way of conveying a relationship and often leaves consumers and others questioning the nature of the brand. Moreover, connecting two brands raises issues about what each adds to the other. If one brand is radical and challenging and the other conservative and unquestioning, we might wonder about the nature of the partnership. On the other hand if the brands have similar or complementary values then the partnership may have a synergistic effect. The argument for linkage again comes back to what each brand adds to the other. Employees also read these connections. If they feel that the co-brand bolsters their sense

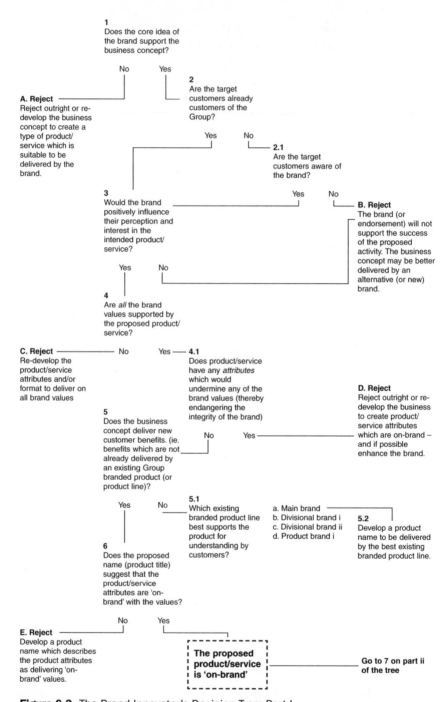

Figure 6.3 The Brand Innovator's Decision Tree: Part I

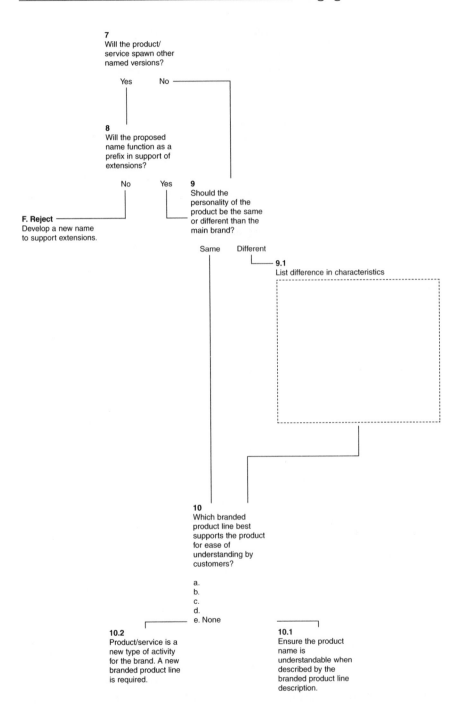

Figure 6.3 The Brand Innovator's Decision Tree: Part II

of esteem they are more likely to be positive than if it in some sense undermines their sense of worth or challenges their identity. For example, the employees of a highly creative company might feel deeply uncomfortable with an alliance with a systems-led company because they feel it would constrain their ability to be creative and also because it might undermine their standing with their peer groups. Similarly, there will be fears if the company decides to license its name to others. The loss of control over operational delivery has the potential to damage a brand, even when licensing, makes business sense. To use the brand in this way there needs to be clarity as to the values and there also need to be clear service-level agreements to which everyone adheres.

Extranets

As the boundaries between the inside and the outside of the organization blur, so the need for a clear understanding of the brand broadens. The increasing prevalence of networked organizations means many different organizations and people are involved in communicating the brand idea. This is particularly important in the automotive industry, where dealerships that are independently owned are prime determinants of brand image. Although the manufacturer can exert some influence in terms of standards of performance, it is far more powerful, if the dealer understands the brand idea and is capable of delivering it effectively. This suggests that a brand education programme and training mechanisms need to be put in place. While personal interaction is an important component in this, building an extranet that can involve dealers in the development of the brand and the active sharing of good brand ideas can only enhance the development of the organization's image. With their direct interaction with customers, dealers are particularly well placed to input into this. An extranet can also engage upstream suppliers whose component quality and service input will also determine the strength of the brand. This networked approach to the brand recognizes that while each individual component of the service or product delivery is independent, from the consumer perspective the brand is a unified entity. It will do the automotive manufacturer little good to blame a failing in the product to the gearbox manufacturer or the quality of servicing from the dealer.

Branding on the Internet

The content and navigation of some Web sites indicates that companies can all too easily separate the brand experience on the Web from other forms of delivery. Generally the customer will not see it this way. The Web is another form of communication. Thus the presentation on the Web should be built around the organizational brand idea, while using the unique attributes of interactivity and community building that the Web provides. To evaluate the quality of match between the physical and electronic brand it is possible to conduct a brand healthcheck.[5] The healthcheck uses qualitative research to establish how customers and potential customers view a brand and its competitors. The research involves the assessment of brand expectations based on the physical experience and the degree to which expectations are met or exceeded by the electronic experience. It is also possible to evaluate how well the attributes of the Web are used. Each interviewee's on-screen moves are filmed, as are facial expressions. This provides a reference source that can pinpoint general issues, such as the positioning of the brand relative to others and specific issues, such as failures in the navigation process.

The other aspect that communication professionals need to engage with is that, although it may be easy to agree to the principles of interaction and community building, databases and systems need to be sufficiently well developed to provide personalization and the logistics support. The success of Amazon as an online retailer is in no small part due to the fact that it has developed software that is particularly effective in terms of human computer interaction (HCI). It has enabled customers to review books and rate book reviews, it publishes rankings based on purchasing data, it recommends titles and it facilitates links by analysing a customer's clickstream. These and other innovations moved *The Economist* to comment that 'could it be that the most accurate way to describe the firm is as a software company, rather than a retailer?'[6] In contrast, the very public demise of Boo.com (the online sportswear retailer) was due to failings in software and logistics. Thus the external marketing of the company via the Web cannot occur before the operational functions are effective.

As well as the functionality issues described above, there is also the issue that customers see the Web as a proxy for the people behind the company. This is true for all non-human interactions, because we believe that decisions about these interactions reflect assumptions about customers. One example of this is Trailfinders. Ring up Trailfinders and you get the inevitable recorded message – in itself a source of irritation. However, whereas other companies simply inform you that you are in a queue and leave you to comtemplate endlessly repetitive playings of Greensleeves, Trailfinders tell you your position in the queue, the speed with which enquiries are being dealt with and the estimated time until your call is answered. This is constantly updated – with reasonable accuracy – until your call is answered. Normally, even when you are number 15 in the queue, the answering time is no more than four minutes. A more frustrating example was a tour operator, which told me I was first in the queue, but still took 25 minutes to answer the call. My reading of Trailfinders is that it is an organization that treats your custom seriously.

Thus, although the Web may appear to be simply another means of delivery, it can and does convey ideas about the brand and the employees of the company. This aspect is heightened, if the Web is supported by chat rooms, where employees and customers come together to engage in conversation, or if the Web is linked to a call centre. Here the continuity of experience is vital: the Web should not indicate one thing about the company and a call centre another. The tone of voice should be the same.

The primary benefit for organizations in this opening up of the brand to the outside world is that can help differentiate it and it can generate trust. With so many companies offering broadly similar products and services there is a real concern with how to differentiate them. Unless there is a genuine and sustainable business concept innovation one of the keys to differentiation will be the same as in the physical world: people. Similarly, as research by the Internet consultancy Sapient & Cheskin Research (1999) demonstrates, there is a clear need for Web companies to build trust with their consumers. Their findings suggest there are six key factors in generating trust:

- brand;
- navigation;
- fulfilment;
- presentation;
- up-to-date technology;
- logos of security guaranteeing firms.

It can be seen that all of the above contribute to a consumer's idea of brand. For the people who develop and maintain the Web and provide the operational support, it is important that the brand idea steers their approach.

As with advertising, employees are an important audience of the organization's Web site. It is a signal to the outside world and therefore creates a focus for supportive behaviour. If the tone of the Web site conveys the notion that the organization is professional and passionate it will be a spur to employees to sustain the idea. Equally, if the Web site is staid and corporate, yet the organization is hip and cool, employees will tend to feel that the site is not relevant and they may even disparage it to others – 'we're not as dull as the Web site makes out'. The accuracy of the Web mirror is important for self-esteem, but also given the prevalence with which organizations use their Web sites as a promotion for recruitment, it may do them a disservice externally. The Web site ought to be a clear reflection of the brand that works for both the knowledgeable visitor and the browser.

Summary

Brand programmes have little relevance if they simply define a set of words that everyone, apart perhaps from the marketing department, ignores. To move from words into meaning the brand needs to acquire substance; to affect the organization's performance. There are a number of mechanisms that can help achieve this, including, brand books, games, workshops, promotional items, brand champions, intranets and extranets. All of these can help to embed and then sustain the idea. However, management needs to set an example and live the brand more overtly than others – this will provide a signal to employees that the brand idea is seen as an important aspect of organizational performance. This will help to overcome the cynicism that exists in pockets in many organizations.

Continuing the theme of the previous chapter there is also a strong argument for making all of the suggested activities as participative as possible. The more top-down the approach the harder it is to build genuine commitment to the brand. The eventual goal should be to move the brand from the conscious to the intuitive so that people no longer have to think about the brand but simply know the right thing to do. This will not happen overnight, especially if the brand implies a significant change in attitude, but it should nonetheless be the aim.

Notes

1 Pfeffer, Jeffrey (1998) *The Human Equation*, Harvard Business School Press, Boston, MA, p 140.
2 Hargadon, Andrew and Sutton, Robert (2000) Building an innovation factory, *Harvard Business Review*, (May–June), p 157–66.
3 MacKenzie, Gordon (1998) *Orbiting the Giant Hairball*, Viking Penguin, Harmondsworth, p 205.
4 Greyser, Stephen, 'Corporate image and the bottom line', speech at the launch of the International Corporate Identity Group, House of Lords, 24 January 1996.
5 The brand Healthcheck is a registered trademark of Icon Medialab.
6 Amazon, the software company, *The Economist* (14 October 2000), p 80.

seven

Sustaining **the brand: stories and myths**

Stories and myths about how the organization dealt with key competitors in the past, how it survived a downturn in the economy, how it developed a new and exciting product, how it dealt with a valued employee, and so on, not only spell out the basic mission and specific goals (and thereby reaffirm them) but also reaffirm the organization's picture of itself, its own theory of how to get things done and how to handle internal relationships.[1]

There is a need to sustain the brand over time. This requires something that personalizes the idea of the brand so that it attains a vitality that motivates employees and builds identification with the organization's cause. While hard facts, research and performance data are helpful signals of the success of the brand and can deepen commitment, there is real value in a more qualitative source of inspiration: storytelling. This is an activity that people and organizations engage in naturally. It does not need to be forced. However, it can be focused and harnessed so that the stories really help to build the brand idea. It can help to stir employees' imaginations about the organization they work for and it can act as a bonding agent, so that people from different competencies within the organization can share a common view of the world. Think for a moment of any religion and the power of its stories. In Christianity, biblical parables are the things that people remember and it is the interpretation of these that hold the faith together. Such is the power of these stories that historically the Church has tried to maintain control over the interpretation of meaning, dismissing alternative ideas as blasphemy. This thought control is not viable within a corporate context, but the value of stories should not be underestimated. This becomes even more noticeable when organizations grow rapidly and/or geographically or when there is a rapid turnover of staff. In the past, in most organizations, there was sufficient stability for natural storytellers to emerge and to create disciples. Now the degree of flux means that organizational amnesia can happen all too quickly. An organization sets up, grows to a few thousand people in a few years, the founders take advantage of their new found wealth generated by their IPO and leave, the business professionalizes its operations and the few remaining early appointees become disenchanted and decide to set up on their own to recapture the excitement of those early years. Now there's no one around to remember the important decisions or what the culture was really like or what the vision and values actually mean. To help build continuity and to link the past with the present and the future, stories need to be captured and disseminated.

Why stories?

Connecting to the past

Sometimes we can look at an old school photograph and realize that we have not only forgotten the names of most of our classmates, but that we cannot even relate to the image of ourselves. Who is that person who looks out of the photograph? What did they really think? The only way we can connect to that past is by remembering events and recreating stories about our experiences. Now think about the organization you work for. If it has any history, the only way you can truly connect to its past is through the stories that have probably entered corporate legend. The potential difficulty here is that if the stories are simply descriptive of the past the personalities involved will have a two-dimensional quality. It is only when we see the thinking and emotional person in the story that we can make connections with our current lives. One of the interesting facets of advertising agency, Leo Burnett's brand statement, is that it was culled from the papers, memos and sayings of Leo Burnett himself. As one of the values says, 'as if Leo were looking over our shoulders'. This personalization helps us relate to Leo Burnett rather than imagining him as some behatted ad man in a black and white photograph. Similarly at Nike, the character of Bill Bowerman, who was one of the founders of the company, looms large through his sayings and the stories that epitomize his uncompromising attitude to athletics and business.

Articulating our own experiences

The very best stories seem to convey experiences we can relate to, more powerfully than we could articulate the experience ourselves. If a story is well told or written we engage with it because we can identify our idea of self in the story but we probably recognize that we couldn't have expressed it as well. This relates to the experience of reading a story and the reflective attitude it encourages. We see ourselves in the characters and we begin to share their ideas but we are also transported into a deeper experience, because a strong story will bring to the fore thoughts that have been locked in the back of our mind and that we have never articulated. We can then become more aware of our surroundings and sensitive to associations we had never before recognized. In this book, for example, I have used stories from Gordon MacKenzie's book *Orbiting the Giant Hairball* to convey ideas. His stories are valuable because they provide engaging and involving narratives that reinforce our own experiences and stimulate our imagination.

Here's another one that brings back memories of all the times I've lacked the courage to do the sensible thing. MacKenzie relates the story of visiting a cliff face near San Diego and being confronted by a series of signs 'DANGER!' 'STAY BACK! UNSTABLE CLIFFS', 'NO BEACH ACCESS'. However, when he looked over the cliff edge, he could see a beach some two hundred feet below with people sunbathing. It looked appealing. It didn't seem that dangerous. He stepped over the chains and past the signs. Having negotiated the first 120 feet by sliding down, he reached a trough beyond which he couldn't see the way down. He moved to the edge and then panicked and moved back. He just couldn't tell what lay below. Nor could he now get back up the cliff again. He was too embarrassed to call out so he decided to just sit and wait. Eventually the crowd on the beach noticed his position and someone called to find out why he was there. He had to admit he was stuck. His legs began to shake. Rescuers were called and some 40 minutes later the Sheriff's helicopter appeared and winched him to safety with a polite but firm reprimand, of which he says, 'emotionally, I regressed to age six.' Back in the hotel room that evening he mused on his adventure:

> I thought of how – even though, intellectually, I realize that all of us experience impasse many times in our lives – I had found it so difficult to say that I was stuck. It requires a certain courage to make such an admission…
>
> Ah! Courage, courage, courage. Courage to cross boundaries. Courage to admit idiocy. Courage to acknowledge impasse. Courage to open up to being rescued. We need much courage if we are to respond successfully to the consequences of exploring beyond authorities' sometimes-beneficial, sometimes-detrimental boundaries. And if we are to grow, explore we must.[2]

MacKenzie's story is reminiscent of Thomas Hardy's, *A Pair of Blue Eyes* (1873), where the main character, Henry Knight, falls over a cliff edge and is rescued by the heroine, Elfride. Both narratives contain essential storytelling elements. They contain an initial element of foolhardiness that precipitates the crisis. They are both told from a single narrative viewpoint, which helps to maintain the focus of the reader and the identification with the characters. They both have an element of suspense in that they pose the question of what will happen next and then delay the answer.

Inspiration

Stories can also inspire us, because they represent a world where others possessed of more courage than ourselves do things that we half imagine we are capable of but in reality recognize we could not. Most of the time we avoid making difficult decisions because we avoid the anxiety that inevitably accompanies such choices.

Through stories we can admire a leader who confronts a difficult situation, organizations that stick to their principles come what may or an employee who has the courage to tell management what it's doing wrong. We can make statements about these actions, but it is through the example of a story that we can begin to visualize the concepts and find things to emulate. When we are then confronted by similar situations we do not have to ask 'what is the guiding principle here?' We can use the story as a reference point. We might even ask, what would Leo have done? In the story-rich world of Patagonia, stories seem to come from everywhere: employees, customers, suppliers and sports people. However, it is the charismatic Yvon Chouinard, who really defines the organization. In response to the question 'where does Patagonia's opinionatedness come from?' creative director, Hal Arneson, says:

> Yvon. Ask me any of these things and I'll say Yvon to a certain degree. A lot of this is a direct reflection of the person that started the company. And that's not to say the company can't exist without him, but what he brought to this is that characteristic of leadership. He's not afraid at all to express his opinions. Part of my job early on was to try to understand that well enough to create documents to say what is it that guy has inside him that we can emulate. There's a certain amount of translation that goes on. You have to know when to take what he says literally and when to treat it as a parable.

Memorability

For those with an analytical mind, the power of anecdotes and stories can seem dangerously overrated. They would argue that the experience of an individual is no substitute for understanding how people think collectively. This is true. Stories do not replace the quantitative analysis of opinions and ideas, but they do have the power to stick in our minds. This is because they ask us to participate. Stories do not provide solutions but they do give us insight. Statistical analysis may ask us to think about the implication of data but stories encourage us to use our imaginations and the ones that stimulate us the most become stored, ready for future reference. There are two reasons for this. First, to relate to information we need to be able to contextualize it. For example, if we learn, perhaps through the intranet, that our organization has made a commitment to promoting more innovative products, we might conclude 'that's an interesting development' and go on drinking our coffee. Alternatively the company might narrate an instance in which a committed individual had battled for years against the system to generate an entirely new idea that has proven to be highly successful. As a result the organizational structure has been changed, making it easier for everyone to innovate. Immediately we can relate to the experiences of the people involved and we can imagine what things might be like in future. Perhaps we can see that product idea we've been nurturing for years making an impact. The storyline has engaged us and as a result we remember its message. Secondly, narrative is how we 'rationalize the meaning of our lives as well as dedicate ourselves to long term goals.'[3] Consequently when we hear stories, we have the potential to remember them if they relate to our own personal narratives. Indeed a strong story can literally change our lives, if it causes us to reappraise the meaning of life or our goals.

A word of warning

While stories can be highly influential, there is a danger with them. They can be subject to different interpretations. While the organization might believe that a story epitomizes the brand values, employees might see other nuances or read the story in exactly the opposite way. The way that different people or groups can read the same narrative in different ways is brought to light by *Stories of Scottsboro* (Goodman, 1995). In this book, Goodman narrates an incident that occurred during the depression when nine black teenagers were seized from a train in Alabama and accused of the rape of two white women who were travelling as hoboes along with the blacks. There was no medical sign of rape yet the blacks were convicted and sentenced to death. The sentences were never carried out but there were a series of retrials. One of the strands that Goodman develops is that both the whites and blacks of

Alabama defined coherent narratives from the perceived facts of the case to support their respective ideas of what happened. Neither side could imagine how the other could possibly hold a different view.[4] *Scottsboro* demonstrates that we approach stories from a particular cultural perspective and that we attach our own meaning to events. In a corporate context, the greater the degree of organizational identity the more likely it is that people will read a story in a similar way; that they will uncover the same meaning. Papa, Auwal and Singhal in a study of the Grameen Bank in Bangladesh note that 'When members identify strongly with an organization, they only see decision options that are consistent with organizational values. They do not question these values because they have internalised them.'[5]

However, the larger the organization and the greater the diversity within it, the more likely there will be alternative readings of a story. Where there is lower organizational identification there will be higher variability in interpreting the meaning. This is not necessarily a bad thing. Academic institutions and non-governmental organizations in particular tend towards individualistic interpretations because they are used to questioning. However, in these organizations there is always a greater danger of individualism overtaking the sense of group. Part of the trade off for joining a group – whether it is a business or a sports team or a faculty – is some subsuming of individualism in the pursuit of collective success.

Depending on the strength of organizational identification, there will be more or fewer opportunities for different interpretations of a story. This happens with any narrative form. Thus, the story of managerial confrontation with a union might look like strength to some and bluster to others. The greater the unity between individual and corporate values, the more the likelihood that the employee reading of the story will be the same as the organization. However, in organizations where there are contrary views, there are difficulties with the overt use of stories as a mechanism. There will be a tendency to see stories as something manipulative rather than expressions of identity. The inference is that in diverse organizations any story that seeks to bolster the organizational values needs to be carefully considered and read from different perspectives before wider dissemination.

Effective stories

The prime requirement of a story is that it should relate to organizational goals. There will always be stories circulating among employees and, as Van Riel says, 'stories are vital to sense-making within organizations.' However, the stories will not necessarily be positive nor will they automatically sustain the key ideas of the organization. Although, as suggested, one can nurture stories, storytelling is a democratic process. Anyone can tell a story and if the story is good it will have the potential to gain wide acceptance. Stories are not controllable – there may be instances of corporate excess for example, which become popular because they seem to define a go-getting, hedonistic atmosphere. It can be fun to revel in these stories but ultimately they may not be effective. Generally, the more authentic and widely shared the values the greater the likelihood that stories will be supportive. In some voluntary organizations, where a cause can be strongly and widely supported, there is often a clear continuity in the storytelling.

Van Riel also argues that effective stories should have two key elements: credibility and novelty. Credibility relates to the authenticity of the story. Is it real? Is it central to what the organization does? Is it supported by other organizational messages? Novelty, as Van Riel describes it, relates to the potential for differentiation. How does the story demonstrate that this organization is different from others? The more distinctive the story, the more it defines the individuality of corporate members. It says we're not the same as others. I would also add another element to this idea of novelty. Stories can illustrate consistent themes – this is an outcome of consistent values. However, as employees change over time, they need new variants of stories and to see new nuances. An employee who has been with an organization for five years is not the same person as the one that joined straight from college. Work and life experience will have changed them. The old stories will perhaps become stronger for long-serving employees as they act as a bonding mechanism for those that remain and can recall the past. New stories will be read differently. If the organization's atmosphere is positive they will have potentially more power as they add new layers of meaning to the work experience. The alternative scenario is where the organization's members become more cynical over time and come to distrust stories.

The nature of stories can vary, but they reflect the structures that appeal to people in general. In fact research by Martin, Feldman, Hatch and Sitkin[6] shows the remarkable similarity in organizational stories. The struggle of the hero against the odds is powerful, because it shows the potential of people for self-actualization. It also stresses the importance of clear thinking and perseverance. Companies inevitably have their ups and downs and it is important that employees know that the organization has struggled through hard times in the past and successfully weathered the storm. In storytelling, whether it is in films, plays or novels, adversity is an important element, not only because it reminds us of our humanity and that success cannot be taken for granted, but also the experience is cathartic and makes the resolution all the more powerful. As Nietzsche suggests, we should not avoid difficult experiences, because they define what we are as individuals. A variant on the epic is the version of the romantic drama. Here the organization loses its direction because it is untrue to its beliefs but rediscovers itself through organizational learning. The appeal here is that the storyline reflects our desire for truth and the discomfort we feel when we disappoint ourselves. We can then degenerate further if we become self-pitying, but if we return to our true selves and learn the lessons of failing we end up as more rounded characters. As with all stories there needs to be forces of evil that threaten the purity of the organization or its epic journey. Homer's adventures of Odysseus needs Circe, Cyclops and the Sirens as a juxtaposition to the actions of Odysseus. His confrontations enable him to grow in knowledge and stature. Equally Nike needed Adidas, Apple needed IBM and Virgin needed British Airways. Each of these organizations defined themselves by what they were not, such that Apple when it launched the Macintosh, created a 1984 world in which automotons sat in rapt silence in front of a giant television screen featuring Big Brother (at the time a proxy for IBM) until a runner appears and smashes the screen. The take out was that IBM was trying to control but Apple was going to empower people – computing for everyone.

Storytelling at Nike

Nike is an organization that lives on stories. Like Patagonia, the nature of its origins in sport create a fertile breeding ground for swapping anecdotes with other like-minded, passionate people. In the early days of the organization this happened as a natural consequence of an organization that was created in the mould of a running team. Nike's founders, Bill Bowerman, who was a track coach at the University of Oregon and Phil Knight, one of his runners, believed in the importance of commitment and teamwork and these ideas drove the company forward. This helped to create an organizational culture that was freewheeling, entrepreneurial, highly collaborative and very flat. Anybody could do anything because there was so much to do and nobody knew what to do. People would be selected on the basis of 'you show some tendencies for being a good manager, so why don't you go and run the footwear division?' Nike attracted people who loved sport – mostly they were runners or ex-runners – who really didn't want to work at a real job. Rather they wanted to work for a cause – and the cause was running.

Bill Bowerman taught the athletes that ran for him to be competitive and to learn to win. When it came to business he adopted the same spirit. At the time Adidas was the most powerful sports company in the world. The Olympic teams and the athletes all wore Adidas. Yet Bowerman and Knight understood sports and athletes and they wanted to win. Within 10 years Nike was a serious rival and in 15 it surpassed Adidas. In part this was because Adidas didn't understand the American jogging boom – it thought it was just a fad. In Germany runners would go to a track and run around it. In the United States, runners became joggers. In part it was because of the culture of Nike and the passion of its people.

Nelson Farris, Chief Storyteller at Nike and employee number 18, says:

> When you ran track for Bowerman, you did absolutely the best you could every time. When you push yourself constantly you recognize that if you don't do your single best for you, you also let the team down. From that, when I came to work at Nike I

sensed this team thing. It meant that if you made a commitment and you told your buddy you were going to do something, you wouldn't let a friend down. The teamwork was powerful. Phil Knight understood it and the first employees, who were ex-Bowerman athletes, understood it. They taught us by their actions: if a guy said he was going to do something; he would do it every time. You'd never hear excuses – people came through for each other – consistently. As a result we just started doing things. If people tried and failed, no problem, we'd just come at it again. That's a part of learning – failing like crazy. We were all terrified we were going to go broke, because we were such a small company. But we innovated and experimented. We'd listen to runners, go and try things out and sometimes come back within 24 hours and let the runner use it. So through that listening, that instantaneous feedback, through taking risks and trying to invent product we were able to do things way different from anybody else.

Examples of this commitment and learning abound within the Nike store of tales. When the company started Bowerman would shave any excess leather off runners' shoes. He calculated that every ounce shaved off a miler's shoe equated to 200 fewer pounds carried in the race. Nike's first employee, Jeff Johnson, sold shoes by going to track meetings, talking to runners, understanding their needs and building them prototypes. Nike supported Steve Prefontaine, the American Olympic runner, in his attempts to make running a professional sport. Each of these stories demonstrates where Nike's soul is: in running and fitness. This idea of a cause was not formally articulated but people within the company talked about it. This worked when the company was small and people knew each other, but by the late 1970s, when the company moved from hundreds to thousands of people, it needed to be formalized. People who hadn't grown up with Bowerman and the sports-obsessed culture couldn't comprehend the idea of going for a 12-mile run before work nor the very distinct belief in teamwork. As a result the company started to try to analyse its own culture and to define what it truly believed in. It started with a one-hour programme on the organization and its beliefs; by the mid-1980s it was a one-day programme and by the 1990s it was a three-day programme. The company also restructured. In becoming big it recognized that it had lost some of the intimacy it had when it was small. Consequently it created 300 mini-Nikes. All the different divisions had to be built into small units that would be completely focused and motivated while still remaining connected to the ultimate mission and the values.

Nike values

In the early 1990s Nike decided to formalize its values. It did a survey of its employees and then encouraged people to input their ideas on the expression of the values. The ideas came from the long servers, like Farris, and also the newcomers. The goal was to focus on as few words as possible. Originally 12 value words were shortlisted, but through debating the nuances of the words they shrunk to three: honest, competitive and teamwork. Behind each of the words are supporting ideas. For example, 'honest' means that people respect each other's opinions; if someone makes a mistake they accept responsibility and it means that Nike aims to make authentic athletic products for athletes. 'Competitive' means that Nike aims to win, to be the best, to be the most innovative and to be a risk taker. 'Teamwork' is recognizing that to make a contribution to the collective you do your best individually; it is understanding that people need each other to be their most effective.

Once the company had its values agreed, it needed to embed them. Part of the process involves the mechanisms that have been mentioned in this book, but the idea of storytelling is elevated to a key component in sustaining the brand. Nelson Farris's role is to explain the evolution of the culture to employees and to underpin the values. This involves using stories, both good and bad, to capture the overall essence of the company. The stories can be from the distant or the recent past. Farris argues that the continuity of the brand means that the themes in the stories keep repeating themselves. Although it could be argued that there is a self-consciousness about the management of storytelling, Farris says the company has always told stories from Bill Bowerman and the waffle iron to the design of the Goatek:

> The company has been a storytelling company from day one – when we make something, somebody writes a draft and it's a one-page story. For example the one pager will say we're going to make a soccer shirt. The story behind this is in 1994 we

signed the Brazilians to wear Nike soccer boots. When the Brazilians played the Americans, they swapped their jerseys at the end. A Brazilian player takes his old nylon jersey off and it's full of sweat and the American has this stuff called Dry Fit – a polyester woven material that whips all the moisture away. The Brazilians said to their coach, 'why can't we have these'. So we worked on a new fabric. The one pager was the story of the Brazilians versus the Americans and the brief was to design a new fabrication that reduces the weight and increases the cooling properties. So literally we tell stories about everything we do. That's how we present to people.

Another area of storytelling for Nike is the tales of conflict within the organization. This comes through strongly in a 1991 biography of the company called _The Unauthorized Story of Nike and the Men who Played There._[7] At one level this could be a criticism of Nike, but the company would argue that confrontation is good: you can argue and fight if you believe in the corporate cause and if you trust your colleagues. It also relies on a non-hierarchical structure, where people can express their opinions, whatever their position. Although this was true of the early days of the organization, as the company has grown the development of hierarchy can now get in the way. Part of the value of the early stories about confrontation is that the openness and passion show a different way of thinking – one where hierarchy is denied. Nelson Farris says:

> Conflict has always been part of Phil Knight's philosophy – and he believes if you really have passion and you really believe in what you're doing then you put all the argument necessary to sell your idea. If you don't have passion you won't be able to stand up to someone else that has greater passion and motivation.

The right stories

Stories do not have to be true to be valid. Delve deep into the history of most organizations and you can find that the facts have been adapted to meet the needs of a more powerful story. Even when people are confronted with the real events they will try to argue for the corporate myth as truth. Rather than questioning the validity, it is better to accept the perception of truth. What is important is that the stories have to be true to the spirit of the organization and they therefore have to be based on the brand and what it stands for. For Nike, the concept of 'irreverence justified' promotes the brand as focusing on performance improvement and an in-your-face attitude; the combination of emotion and function. Consequently Nike stories perpetuate these ideas. Consumers may buy the products because they think the clothes and shoes are cool, but within Nike the storytelling is focused on the athlete as consumer and the attempts of the company to meet their needs. The stories can encompass failure, as this is the accepted by-product of innovation, but they should also demonstrate Odyssean perseverance.

Stories should also reflect the everyday interests of employees. In a technical environment, employees may want to talk about the engineering of a particular item, but in a consumer-oriented company most power comes through product usage and the stories associated with it. This suggests the importance of knowing your employee audience and being able to connect with them effectively. This is easier within organizations such as Nike, Patagonia and UNICEF, where the cause is clear to all. The harder task is within organizations where there is less clarity about the brand. The inference is that the brand needs to be defined and understood before using storytelling as a mechanism to encourage engagement. As Farris reminds us:

> When you are able to blend this (your work) with your life then you're just rich with stories. You don't go home and talk about the dual density of the running shoe, you talk about some athlete wearing your stuff and setting a world record.
>
> I think storytelling is an informal process of communicating that humans want to do, because that's what they do when they're around their friends and family. We create a storytelling environment – it's just the way we talk. You're trying to figure out a process to get adults to learn and to get adults to change. The more you understand – and you understand more by listening to the stories – the easier it is to go 'aah: transition over'.

Summary

Storytelling is the way that communities share and preserve their heritage. Stories explain the nature of organizational life and sustain knowledge. It is through stories that a culture is built. Thus the mechanism of storytelling is the most powerful way to embed a brand in the organization. To some this might seem a self-conscious attempt at employee manipulation but it should not involve the creation of invented narratives. Rather it is about capturing the stories that best support the brand idea and then nurturing them through retelling. Not all organizations will want to employ someone who has a remit to tell stories, but the telling of stories should be built into corporate education programmes and the skills of storytellers should be promoted through training and providing the material to help the process. This will help to encourage attitudes and behaviour that are more in tune with the brand. This suggests an important facet of storytelling, for while stories relate past events, what they attempt to do is influence our future actions and to change the way we see ourselves and those around us. An example of this occurring within a story is this rhythmic narrative about the epiphany of a young man as he watches a girl wade into the sea. It confirms his future resolve to be an artist rather than the priest:

Her slateblue skirts were kilted boldly about her waist and dovetailed behind her. Her bosom was as a bird's soft and slight, slight and soft as the breast of some darkplummed dove. But her long fair hair was girlish: and girlish, and touched with the wonder of mortal beauty, her face....Her image had passed into his soul for ever and no word had broken the holy silence of his ecstacy. Her eyes had called him and his soul had leaped at the call. To live, to err, to fall, to triumph, to recreate life out of life!'[8]

Notes

1 Schein, Edgar (1985) *Organizational Culture and Leadership*, Josey-Bass, San Francisco, CA, p 80.
2 MacKenzie, Gordon (1998) *Orbiting the Giant Hairball*, Viking Penguin,

Harmondsworth, p 80.

3 Barresi, John (1999) On becoming a person, *Philosophical Psychology*, **12**, pp 79–98.

4 Cited in Barresi, John (1999) On becoming a person, *Philosophical Psychology*, **12**, pp 79–98.

5 Cited in Whetten, David and Godfrey, Paul (eds) (1998) *Identity in Organizations: Building Theory Through Conversations*, Sage, London, p 264.

6 Martin J, Feldman M, Hatch MJ, Sitkin S (1983) The uniqueness paradox in organizational stories, *Administrative Science Quarterly*, **28**, pp 438–53.

7 Strasser, JB and Becklund, Laurie (1991) *The Unauthorized Story of Nike and the Men who Played There*, Harcourt Brace Jovanovich, New York.

8 Joyce, James (1977) *Portrait of the Artist as a Young Man*, Panther Books, St Albans, Herts, p 156.

eight

Measuring **success**

To help confront the cynicism about the value of brands within organizations there needs to be systems of measurement that demonstrate the benefit of undertaking what can be expensive and time-consuming programmes. Indeed if a brand is to achieve real status, there needs to be an ongoing commitment to sustaining and evaluating it over time. As Matthew Bell, Communications Director of VSO notes, the most difficult task is persuading fellow managers that a brand can deliver real bottom line benefits.

One of the best-known measures of brand value is Interbrand Newell and Sorrell's brand valuation analysis. Working from publicly available information, such as annual reports, analysts' reports, trade journals and industry analyses, each year Interbrand publishes a league table of brand values. This work covers major global organizations and shows that some organizations achieve more than three quarters of their market capitalization from their brands and that overall 20 per cent to 30 per cent of stock market capitalizations are derived from brands. Interbrand defines the brand as an asset in terms of such factors as trademark rights and patents, research and development, customer databases, distribution and expertise. It is the brand that drives customer demand through perceptions of quality, design, features, lifestyle and innovation. The formula used to calculate the brand value looks at the expected future earnings of the branded business, the role of the brand in generating those earnings and the associated risk profile. The strongest of the Internet-based businesses, such as Yahoo and Amazon, make it on to the list, but generally businesses in this area suffer from uncertainty over future earnings. Comparing the 1999 performance versus 1998, the top five performers are given in Table 8.1.

The difficulty with the Interbrand model as a tool for measuring the effects of internal branding programmes is that it gives an

Table 8.1: 1998/1999 performance

		1998 $bn	1999 $bn
1	Coca-Cola	83.5	72.5
2	Microsoft	56.7	70.2
3	IBM	43.8	53.2
4	Intel	30.0	39.0
5	Nokia	20.7	38.5

overall guide to the brand value, which can be monitored over time, but it does not pinpoint the impact of greater employee involvement and commitment. Movements such as Coca-Cola's were due to a product recall, a racial discrimination action by employees and job cuts. Of course, it could be argued that the racial discrimination action is a direct result of a failure to live the brand but the specifics are hidden within the overall brand performance.

A more precise measure of the impact of the brand on employees is to use the scales suggested by Intellectual Capital models. By building up trend data, the developing influence of the brand idea on people's behaviour can be ascertained. The following list of measures is a guide to how measurement can be undertaken, but it should be recognized that cultural and industry differences may require adaptation. For example, the measurement of government, voluntary organization and business employees will be different because the values and the ultimate goals will vary. Using the Human Focus structure, developed originally for the Swedish financial services company Skandia, Edvinsson and Malone[1] suggest the following measures:

- leadership index (percentage);
- motivation index (percentage): both the leadership and motivation indexes are derived from an analysis of the factors that contribute most to the organization's success and profitability. In Skandia's case employee research analysed:
  - satisfied customers;
  - satisfied salespeople;
  - motivated and competent staff;
  - quality assured and effective administrators;

- empowerment index (of 1,000): this was a result of research among employees to determine their sense of control over their work and covered:
  - motivation;
  - support within the organization;
  - awareness of quality demands;
  - responsibility versus authority to act;
  - competence;
- number of employees;
- employee turnover (percentage);
- average years of service with the company;
- number of managers;
- number of women managers;
- average age of employees;
- time in training – days / years;
- IT literacy of staff;
- number of full-time / permanent employees;
- average age of full time / permanent employees;
- average years with company of full-time permanent employees;
- annual turnover of full-time permanent employees;
- per capita annual cost of training, communications and support programs for full-time permanent employees (£);
- full-time permanent employees who spend less than 50 per cent of work hours at a corporate facility;
- number of full-time temporary employees;
- per capita annual cost of training and support programs for full-time temporary employees (£);
- number of part-time employees / non-full-time contractors;
- average duration of contract;
- percentage of company managers with advanced degrees
  - business (%);
  - advanced science and engineering (%);
  - advanced liberal arts (%).

The above measures try to evaluate the degree of commitment and motivation of a workforce, the organizational structure and the capacity to retain and develop employees. These relate to the brand in that achieving identification with the organizational vision and values should lead to increased motivation and employee retention, whereas the structure of the workforce and the commitment to its development reflect management priorities. The benefit to the organization of retention of employees is that the longer people stay with the organization the greater the value they produce. The consultancy Bain & Company has developed a generic model of the economic benefits of employee loyalty, which aptly demonstrates this:

- Recruiting investment. The cost and uncertainty of hiring people makes it more cost effective to retain current employees.
- Training. Training is required throughout a person's career, but the cost of training long-term employees is offset by the training and advice they impart to colleagues.
- Efficiency. Experience aids efficiency. 'As a general rule, employees who stay with the company because they're proud of the value they create for customers and pleased with the value they create for themselves are more motivated and work harder.'[2]
- Customer selection. Experienced sales people and marketers are better at seeking out the best customers.
- Customer retention. Customers build relationships with long-term employees: '...in banking, brokering and auto service, long-term employees create higher customer loyalty. Even in manufacturing, however, where employees rarely meet customers, long-term employees can produce better products, better value for the customers and better customer retention.'[3]
- Customer referral. Loyal employees can be a major source of customer referrals.
- Employee referral. Long-term employees often refer the best quality applicants.

The above again indicates why it is important in the recruitment process to ensure there is a good match of values between the individual and the organization and then over time to nurture the relationship between the two.

Despite the potential benefits of employee retention, one should be careful about praising retention for its own sake. This is not a mandate to retain uninterested people or saboteurs but it is a recommendation to ensure that as many people as possible understand and engage with the organizational brand. The limitation of the intellectual capital model as it stands is that the outputs are one step removed from the impact of the brand idea. Therefore, whereas identification may be a factor in achieving change, it might not be the only one. Motivation of employees might also be due to policies developed independent of the brand. To achieve the necessary link between the brand idea and the impact on people, we need to ascertain the understanding and the effect of the values.

Evaluating brand commitment

To understand how employees see the brand and its relevance to their day-to-day working lives, ongoing research needs to be conducted. This will help to determine the strength and relevance of the brand and pinpoint any areas of weakness. The latter is especially important, if the articulation of the brand is new or if the organization is undergoing significant change. For example, if one of the brand values lacks impact with employees and they find it difficult to use, the research will highlight the lack of awareness and usage. The organization can then decide whether the value is misplaced or if it is seen to be important, whether more attention needs to be paid to encouraging engagement with it. Often, if the value is difficult to use, feedback will already have been obtained through the brand champions network and the brand workshops. The benefit of quantitative research among employees is that the scale of the problem can be seen.

There are several methodologies that can be used to undertake the employee research, but probably self-completion questionnaires delivered either in print or electronic formats are most effective. As with other aspects of the brand the response to the questionnaire will in part be determined by the degree of importance that people attach to the brand idea itself. This is a further argument for adopting a participative approach to brand definition, because it is more likely to raise awareness of the brand and its importance to the organization. To encourage people to complete the form it should be accompanied by a note from a champion, stressing the value of the brand and the benefit of employee feedback. This will be more credible to people if the organization has proven in the past that it both listens to and acts upon the knowledge it acquires from people. Alternatively, if the organization has failed to meet this commitment in the past, cynicism will be higher and response rates will be lower. This suggests a real difficulty in developing brands that employees can engage with in organizations where morale is low. If the anticipation of obtaining sufficient responses is in doubt the alternative of telephone interviews should be considered. In terms of the structure of the questionnaire, the following issues should be covered:

- Profile of the respondent in terms of age, sex, geography, status, competence, length of tenure. The value of profiling is that it helps to define whether responses vary due to such variables as the degree of organizational experience or the sort of job that people do.
- The nature of the organizational purpose. This can be either spontaneous or prompted, but it helps to define whether the core purpose statement has been transmitted effectively.
- The key differentiator for the organization. This relates back to the comparative element of the brand definition.
- Describing the organization. Using scalar measures that position opposing values enables the organization to see how well it is performing in the delivery of its values. For example, if the values are innovative, professional, teamwork and challenging, the following polarities might be offered and people asked to score how well the organization performs in living them.

Anti-values	Values
Old-fashioned	Innovative
Amateurish	Professional
Individualistic	Teamwork
Complacent	Challenging

Alongside the specified organizational values, other value words should be included, both to mask the focus on the chosen value words and to establish whether there are words or ideas that have been missed out of the brand definition, which may be important, or if there are areas of underperformance. Figure 8.1 shows the measurement of brand values for the voluntary organization, VSO.[4]

An alternative to posing questions with such bald polarities as 'are we a teamwork based or individualistic organization?' is to look for the meaning behind the words. In this case a series of scalar measures

Here are a number of pairs of opposite adjectives either of which could describe VSO. The first pair is 'caring' and 'unconcerned'. On a scale of 1 to 5 where 'caring' is 1 and 'unconcerned' is 5, where would you place VSO?	%	%	%	%	%	
Caring	22	61	15	1	0	Unconcerned
Helps people to realise their potential*	20	52	23	1	1	Inhibits individuals' development
Open to learning*	15	54	26	3	0	Dogmatic
Patient	15	36	38	7	1	Impatient
Professional & Accountable*	11	58	24	5	0	Amateurish & Undisciplined
Passionate*	11	47	34	6	0	Lukewarm
Adaptable*	7	47	36	7	2	Rule-bound
Focuses on solutions	6	43	45	4	1	Dwells on problems
Keep their promises	6	47	44	2	0	Let people down
Cost effective*	2	20	47	24	3	Wasteful of resources
Innovative*	1	54	36	7	0	Old fashioned
Fast moving	1	12	62	21	1	Slow to respond

* Elements within the brand idea

Figure 8.1 VSO brand values

under the banner 'teamwork' might be explored. Statements can then be posited about aspects of teamwork and individualism in such areas as the attitudes of management, the way problems are solved, the way different competencies work together, the manner of reward systems, the nature of horizontal communication processes and the way employees work with customers. This will give the researcher an insight into the saliency of teamwork and also the specific meaning of the term:

- Understanding the relevance of the brand. The issue here is to determine people's awareness of the role of the brand. These should relate back to the original objectives of the branding programme, but might include:
  - consistency of communication;
  - clarity of communication;
  - building awareness among customers;
  - improving customer service;
  - improving operational standards;
  - increasing sales;
  - enhancing recruitment;
  - improving awareness among financial audiences.
- Views on how well the brand has been communicated. This asks people to pass judgment as to whether the methods – such as the brand book, internal publications and marketing, champions and workshops – have been effective.
- Suggestions on improving internal brand communications. It is important that the answers to this question are segmented in line with the nature of the response to the previous question. This helps to show whether the more negative respondents have the same views as the positive ones. If there is significant variation it may suggest that the message is not getting through to certain parts of the organization. The most common recommendation on improving brand communication is clarity and simplicity, which supports earlier assertions that the brand should be as simply defined as possible.
- The brand as a promise of performance. In an earlier chapter, Feldwick's definition of the brand as 'a promise of performance' was cited. The question here is to what extent does the brand succeed in this respect.
- Impact of the brand on day to day work. This question seeks to uncover the extent to which the brand has had an impact on people's day to day jobs generally and in what areas specifically: this helps to determine how the brand is changing the way people behave within the organization.

- Suggestions on areas of improvement related to the organizational values. This question asks employees to decide which values are delivered best and which need most work.
- Degree of internal integration. This asks people to decide the overall impact of the brand across the organization. This can be supplemented by a question that requires suggestions on areas for improvement. The most frequently cited problem here is the problem of abstraction – employees struggling to see how to use the brand specifically.
- Perception of external image. Much of the above is devoted to people's experience of the organization. However, it is also valuable to know how people believe the organization is seen externally. This can be very influential within the organization, both in terms of people's self esteem and in the impact it has on decision making. The questions in this section should relate to how employees believe they are seen by others (this can require several subquestions depending on the number and nature of external audiences, for example competitors, customers, the media, potential employees) and suggestions as to how the image can be improved.

Undertaking this research is an invaluable guide to the impact of the brand on employees and it helps to identify areas for improvement. However, there are two limitations. *First,* it cannot be a one-off exercise. Without benchmarks it is difficult to gauge the results. It is sometimes possible to conduct research prior to a brand articulation or communication programme, but the difficulty here is that prior to definition it can be difficult to get valid measures. It may be true that the brand idea should draw out concepts already within the organization, but people might not use the terminology that you want to validate later on. What the research can show is the clarity of the articulation and the relative value of the specific elements of the brand idea. Although one can use supplementary qualitative research to uncover employees' views, the real benefit of the research will be shown over time as trend data begin to build. *Second,* the research to this point is all concerned with employee impacts. The brand should have a primary influence on peoples' attitudes within the organization, but living the brand is not about being self-indulgent but rather about delivering benefits to customers and other audiences. Therefore the structure of the employee research should be replicated by external research.

The external perspective

The same methodologies used for employees can be used in the external research. In this instance the key external audiences need to be identified and questionnaires tailored accordingly. The goal here is to obtain an insight into the current perceptions of the organization in terms of the elements of the brand idea and to then check whether there is dissonance between the internal identity and the external image. To achieve this the 12 issues listed in the previous section need to be repeated. Additional to the internal issues, interviewees should be segmented in terms of the nature of their contact with the organization and the length of their relationship. The former point is valuable, because it helps to indicate the primary determinant of their views. Thus the image of the brand could be derived primarily from interaction with employees or from advertising or from the products themselves. The latter point is especially important for organizations that have undergone recent change, as this is more likely to have been felt by people that have come into recent contact, than perhaps by people who have more distantly formed relationships. Research among novice and experienced consumers indicates that these audiences have different information requirements and that experienced consumers of services who have had recent positive experiences are more positive in their evaluations than novice consumers.[5]

Generally, one would anticipate that employees are more aware of the brand and its meaning than external audiences, who may only have a limited awareness of the brand and what it stands for. To provide points of comparison and to help position the organization with reference to others, the external research can also include research into the understanding of key competitors' brands.

The ROIT alternative

An additional methodology to the process outlined above is to use a test, known as ROIT (Rotterdam Organizational Identification Test). The aim of this is to analyse the degree of organizational identification among employees. The test was originally developed at the Corporate Communications Centre at Erasmus University in Rotterdam and has been used extensively among Dutch and Belgian companies.[6] As one of the goals of articulating and embedding the brand idea is to enhance the match between the individual and the organization, ROIT is an appropriate model, not only as a means of evaluating the effects of a brand programme, but also as a means of diagnosis. Thus it can be included within the research methods cited in the process of brand articulation. Its advantage is that it can provide a pre-brand articulation measure of identification, which can then be used as a benchmark for checking future progress. The ROIT involves the administration of a 21-item organizational identification scale that concentrates on such areas as:

- perception of belongingness;
- congruency between organizational goals and personal aims;
- need for affiliation;
- perceived benefit of membership.

The actual test involves employees completing a questionnaire comprising 225 statements. Respondents have to detail on a one-to-five scale their degree of agreement with the statements. The statements fall into five groups: employee communication, perceived organizational prestige, job satisfaction, goals and management style in implementation of goals, corporate culture. The ROIT enables organizations to see the degree to which people identify with the overall organizational brand or their specific team or business unit and the impact of the five areas above on organizational identification. One would hope to see movements in these measures as the brand idea becomes more explicit, but part of the value in the test is in identifying areas that need remedial work. The general finding from ROIT studies is that identification with the business unit will be higher than with the total organization. It has been argued that this occurs because business unit managers strive (as the organization itself does) to enlarge the distinctiveness of the group relative to others. To ascertain the real issues here, Onno Maathuis of Erasmus University in Rotterdam researched this problem, as part of his PhD. His conclusion was that managers identify with their business unit and the organization as a whole, but they identify more strongly with the business unit. However, this identification with the business unit does not impact on their use of the corporate brand.[7]

Another interesting finding of the research carried out using ROIT is that employee communication is a vital component in organizational identification. This posits that there are three factors in employee communication in terms of their impact on identification: the perceived quality of organizational messages; the perceived quality of the communication channels; the quality of the communication climate. However, of these communication climate appears to be the most important. Cees van Riel suggests that:

> how an organization communicates is more important than what is communicated. This stresses the importance of 'soft' aspects in communication like openness, honesty and participation in decision making, resulting in the necessity for managers to pay serious attention to communication climate, specifically their own role in improving the climate.[8]

Analysing the results

Once the results of the internal and external research are available we need to interpret the findings. Some of the issues that might emerge are:

■ Employees and/or external audiences may suggest values that are not included within the original brand definition. This could indicate that there is an element of the original brand idea that has been overlooked or poorly communicated. Action: review the brand definition to determine whether the suggested addition should be included. If the additional element is implicit within the brand idea, then bring it to the fore.

- Certain aspects of the brand, such as one or more of the values may lack impact with people. Action: review the importance of the value or term and ascertain whether it should be discarded or whether more attention should be paid to its promotion.
- The brand has generally failed to penetrate peoples' minds. This suggests a failure of process and/or communication. The brand could be lacking in profile, because it has been imposed from above and employees do not feel engaged with it. Alternatively, there could be a failure to communicate the brand idea to people in a sufficiently powerful way. Action: review the research to establish whether the questions on the relevance and communication of the brand provide insight into the problem. Follow up with qualitative research to get additional depth.
- The brand is well understood (or differently understood) by external audiences relative to internal audiences. If it is better understood, this suggests that the organization has been more effective in promoting the brand in external communications and has probably paid insufficient attention to internal communication. For example, the Dutch bank, Rabobank, conducts annual research into both its identity and image and then compares the fit between the two. Generally the organization finds a good match, but as Karen Beuk, Director of Communications says:'Customers think we are more innovative than we think we are ourselves; on the other hand we think we're very special, but the customers see us as similar to other banks. The crucial measure is "do what you promise". Our customers think we do this better than we do ourselves.' In Rabobank's case the defining break seems to be between head office and branch employees. In the branches, people have more customer contact and therefore have more direct feedback. This tends to encourage a more positive attitude and the bank sees a better match between customer and employee views from this segment of the internal audience. In the case of Rabobank, the recognized solution is to try to enhance communications and improve attitudes, specifically among head office staff. Generally the action point here ought to be to improve internal understanding of the brand idea.
- The brand is well understood (or differently understood) by internal audiences relative to external audiences. This is the opposite of the above and indicates that although the brand has

been effectively embedded into the organization, insufficient attention has been paid to externally communicating the idea. This factor may be due to a time-lag effect, such that employees and marketing communication material are sending out the right brand messages but old perceptions are still pervasive due to the infrequency of interaction with the organization. Action: review the way communications are managed, check the impact of communications against specific external segments and, if necessary, heighten the external communication of the brand.

- There is a good match. Although the overall match might be good, there are always some areas of dissonance. This means that employees can congratulate themselves on a job well done, but challenge themselves to improve in any areas where there are failings.

The brand report

The brand report should be an annual commitment. It should cover all the relevant aspects of the brand, its performance during the year and the goals for the year ahead. The purpose of this report is to keep the brand alive for everyone in the organization (my recommendation is to make this a public document that people within the organization and outside it can share), to stress the benefits of a powerful brand and to identify areas where the brand can be improved. To give the report stature, attention should be paid to both its content and design. The report itself should cover:

- An overview of the performance of the brand.
- The objectives set for the brand overall and by team.
- Examples of the brand in action; showing through storytelling how the brand idea has changed the attitudes and behaviour of individuals and teams. These stories should emerge from within the organization and ideally be written by the individual participants.
- Research statistics from the methods outlined above. Some of this information may be sensitive, but the organization should be as open as possible, especially with its employees. The research should be accompanied by a narrative that explains the implications of the

research and the possible inferences that can be drawn. If any elements of the brand are to be amended the rationale for adaptation needs to well argued – especially if there has been a long and intense process that generated the original definition.

- The impact of the brand on organizational performance. It is sometimes difficult to draw direct parallels with a living the brand programme and the direct impact on sales. However, it is sometimes possible to infer the connection, especially if there is a large number of people within the organization who are directly involved in the process. Certainly it should be possible to draw links between employee retention figures and motivation indices (if these are positive). Another area is recruitment data relating to the number and quality of applicants. Generally the report ought to be careful, about saying, 'as a direct result of articulating our brand' we have seen a 20 per cent increase in sales or a 30 per cent rise in recruitment applications but it should be entirely plausible to argue that 'the clearer articulation of our brand has helped to improve our awareness and we have seen a 30 per cent rise in applications with increasing numbers of people approaching the organization unsolicited.'
- Outlining the objectives for the year ahead. Prior to the publication of the report, the workshop process that generated the previous year's objectives should be iterated so that management and then each team make renewed commitments for the year ahead.

As well as publishing the document for everyone to see, the owners of the brand – whether it be communications or marketing or human resources – should provide a presentation along with a question and answer session on the brand performance and its organizational relevance. As Reichheld has argued, 'employees must know how much value they are creating'.[9]

Summary

There can often be cynicism within organizations about branding, yet the capacity to engage as many people with the idea of living the brand rests on overcoming that cynicism. Anecdotal evidence can be very persuasive, but there is a need to generate robust data that show the pervasive impact a well-articulated brand idea can have on all parts of the organization. The suggestion here is to use a combination of internal and external research to validate the direct impact of the idea both on attitudes and on behaviour. Links can then be made to performance data in such areas as sales, recruitment, employee retention, customer retention and customer satisfaction. This should not be a one-off exercise, but an ongoing commitment to monitoring the performance of the brand. If the knowledge acquired from research is widely shared with employees through a brand report and presentations it can help to pinpoint areas for remedial work and generate renewed commitment to the brand idea. This feedback process stresses the importance of the brand and helps to keep it alive for people.

Notes

1 Edvinsson, Leif and Malone, Michael (1997) *Intellectual Capital: The proven way to establish your company's real value by measuring its hidden brainpower*, Piatkus, London, pp 131–33 and 181–83.
2 Reichheld, Frederick (1996) *The Loyalty Effect*, Harvard Business School Press/Bain & Company Inc, Boston, MA, p 101.
3 Reichheld, Frederick (1996) *The Loyalty Effect*, Harvard Business School Press/Bain & Company Inc, Boston, MA, p 101.
4 The VSO brand statement cites as its core purpose tackling disadvantage by realizing peoples' potential and its values are professional, open to learning, passionate, innovative, adaptable, and cost effective. The research was undertaken one year after the brand definition.
5 Soderlund, Magnus (2000) *Expert and Novice Customers: An examination of perceptions of attribute-level performance*, Stockholm School of Economics, Stockholm.
6 Van Riel, CBM (1995) *Principles of Corporate Communication*, Prentice-Hall, Englewood Cliffs, pp 60–63.
7 Maathuis, Onno (1999) Corporate Branding, PhD thesis, Erasmus University, Rotterdam.
8 Van Riel, Cees (1999) *Ten Years of Research, 1988–1998 of the Corporate Communication Centre, Erasmus University Rotterdam*, Published in the Special Issue on Communication Research in Belgium and the Netherlands, January 27.
9 Reichheld, Frederick (1996) *The Loyalty Effect*, Harvard Business School Press/Bain & Company Inc, Boston, MA, p 126.

nine

Managing **the brand**

There is a seeming simplicity about the ideal of engaging employees with a brand. If we adopt the Maslowian view that individuals are predisposed to seek self-actualization, then all the organization has to do is construct a system that allows for identification with the brand. Yet, predictably there are complexities. Unless the individual is joining a religious order that requires the denial of the self, there cannot be an exact match between personal and corporate aspirations. All that can be hoped for is an approximation. Moreover, given the dynamic nature of both individual and organization, there has to be the recognition that aspirations and identification can change. This is especially true if the identification with a team or business unit dominates the corporate or if there is a major structural change such as a merger or alliance. Then people may start to question or critcize their identification with the brand. The conclusion of this doubt may be that the individual leaves the organization in search of one that is a better match – something that Reichheld points out is damaging to the organization:

> The longer employees stay with the company, the more familiar they become with the business, the more they learn and the more valuable they can be…It is with employees that the customer builds a bond of trust and expectations and when those people leave the bond is broken.'[1]

This problem of alignment of values is a managerial conundrum. Individual values can be moulded to a degree but they cannot be directed. An attempt to move in the direction of the latter creates uncomfortable feelings about manipulation, which we might associate with dictatorial regimes rather than with a business. Although we would want to encourage identification with a corporate brand idea we do not want to deny individuality. Indeed the creativity of individuals should be nurtured. This raises issues of balance: what is a desirable balance between individuality and the group? What is the right level of individual identification? As the economist, Ernst Schumacher, wrote 'we always need freedom and order.'[2]

Individuality

As we saw in the examples of Shakespearean interpretation, individuality is a powerful innovative force. It is the ability of certain people to see things in a different way – to imagine a different future – which creates new ways of doing things. To nurture this imagination in support of a brand there need to be boundaries. Unbridled imagination can be interesting but it does not necessarily benefit the brand. Thus the organization needs to understand itself and to set the context for innovation. The problem here is ensuring that the organization is self-questioning and avoids the dangers of groupthink. Partly this is to do with ensuring that the brand idea itself is sufficiently inspirational and partly this is to do with management of the process. Enabling people to live the brand, requires the organization to generate sufficient order through its processes and systems and sufficient latitude to encourage alternative ways of looking at things. The role of brand champions within the organization is key to this. It is the appointed champions who need to encourage people to look at what they do and to rework their activities in line with the brand. The organization, in turn, needs to make the commitment to help employees restructure what they do. This support should work at the corporate, team and individual levels – all of which should be steered by the brand idea.

At the corporate level there has to be a commitment to recognizing and supporting individualism. This requires the organization to convey the value of individual contributions (as well as the collective) and to allow individuals to challenge the accepted way of doing things. An example of this is Sony's Playstation. It was launched in 1993. Six years later Sony had sold 55 million Playstations and 430 million copies of video game software. Playstation accounted for 40 per cent of the company's $3 billion operating profits in 1999. Yet this product was the result of the hobbyist enthusiasm of one individual within Sony. In the past Sony was defiantly an analogue company, yet one of its engineers, Ken Kutaragi, who joined Sony in the mid-1970s, recognized that the future would be digital. While officially Sony was developing 8 bit MSX computers, Kutaragi was semi-secretly developing 16 bit chips for Nintendo. When this project came out in the open, Kutaragi found himself having to explain himself to the Sony executives. In the end he marshalled enough support to proceed, yet it was some time before the company came to recognize the importance of digital technology and games. It was a lone crusade by one committed and innovative individual that overcame the prejudices of the organization.[3]

In communication terms individualism necessitates a two-way flow of information and ideas and active support for the principles of the brand idea. At the team level, the management task is to enable a dual identification – with both the team and the corporate. The team needs budgets and resources of its own. This enables it to pursue initiatives that emanate from within the team. There should also be sufficient latitude for the team to develop the skill base of its members. Finally at the individual level there should be the opportunity for people to develop their own abilities and knowledge. This again requires funds, but the important point of accountability for the individual and the team is that spending money requires responsibility and accountability to the brand idea.[4] The suggested process here balances freedom and order. It has elements that apply to everyone in the organization but it has elements that focus on the individual. It recognizes that different organizations need (or feel comfortable with) different levels of corporate cohesion and that people have different levels of need to express their individualism. If the organization has been thorough in its recruitment process it will recruit people that match where it sits on the line between collectivist and individual, but there can be no absolutes. There are organizations and nationalities that tend towards individualist and those that tend towards collectivist, but in one direction lies anarchy and the other autarchy.[5] It means that the system for managing the brand needs to be sufficiently flexible to allow collectivists to work comfortably alongside individualists.

Identification

Identification is concerned with the capacity of individuals to identify with an organization and what it stands for. The importance of this for individuals is profound. As we saw in Chapter 3, it defines people's needs for socialization, esteem and self-actualization. Although it is tempting to root identification in time, like other aspects of the individual/corporate relationship it is forever changing. What is the implication for managers of this flux? It is to recognize that as well as the change within an individual over time, different people also need different levels of identification. Some people have a desire to belong to the organization they work for, whereas others have a more detached view and perhaps identify more strongly with a religious body or a social organization. Is there anything wrong with this? In one sense, no – we would probably argue that it is good to have a sense of perspective over the role of work in our lives. However, from the employer's point of view, generally the higher the identification the better as there is a greater potential to turn it into commitment. The difficulty is that identification cannot simply be willed into existence, nor can people be told to identify. Identification comes about when:

- the organization clearly stands for something that is distinctive;
- the organization possesses the emotional intelligence to relate effectively to people's needs;
- the organization communicates a clear message about its beliefs.

Distinctiveness is important because it enhances identification. Research into Christian and Judaic sects shows that the more distinctive the set of beliefs the stronger the emotional identification. The sects achieve this because the distinctiveness of the organization rubs off on the individual. By joining and staying with a clearly defined group, people are making a public statement about their own beliefs. This ties into the third point, which is that the message about beliefs needs to be communicated. People need to understand the cause they are joining and, ideally, they would like others to know the cause as well. Yet, although distinctiveness is good there is a danger of extremes. People mostly want to join organizations that understand their deeper needs and contribute to some degree to the welfare of others. Although I'm not sure it's provable, I would argue that there is a greater appeal and emotional intelligence in becoming, for example, a Quaker rather than a Satanist.

The issue from a management perspective is whether identification can be managed to the right degree. Over-identification can smack of zealotry and be offputting to potential customers,[6] whereas underidentification can seem like lack of interest. Management can reduce the degree of involvement by restricting participation and focusing on systems and can increase it by stepping up the degree of participation. The difficulty here is making this work at the individual level. Although personal counselling and development plans can amend the construct of a participation system so that some have more chance to participate than others, it is difficult radically to alter the balance. As the earlier cited research shows, there are real benefits to more participative approaches and my recommendation is to err on the side of encouraging overidentification, but alongside this to also encourage a questioning attitude. The issue for employees is their options if they choose not to be active identifiers. One can argue that is part of people's personal freedom to decide on their own level of engagement. However, there will tend to be pressures from employers to heighten identification if they perceive benefits from so doing. The key point is how this is achieved. Enthusiasm and persuasion are good, especially if the organization can demonstrate benefits to the individual of identification. Coercion is neither viable nor desirable.

Sitting alongside the virtues of identification with the overall corporate cause are the potential conflicts of identification with a team. Research shows that the immediate identification for most people is connected with a team or business unit rather than with the corporate. This is emphasized when the degree of autonomy increases and reduced when integration with the corporate grows. The goal should always be to ensure that the identification with the team integrates with the identification with the corporate. However, it is a not infrequent experience to come across well-entrenched fiefdoms that brook no outside interference and can actively work against corporate identification. This was an issue with the now merged Grand Metropolitan (currently part of Diageo). Its major division used to be IDV (the drinks and spirits arm of the business). This division was highly successful and possessed a portfolio of powerful brands. However, IDV seemed to dislike being bracketed with other businesses such as foodstuffs and hamburger restaurants and therefore tended to encourage identification with itself at the expense of Grand Metropolitan. This sense of separateness is difficult to overcome if there are strong cultural or strategic differences in the business structure. This may not be important in a conglomerate or in a loose organizational structure, where the corporate brand's main point of accountability is to shareholders. However, when a group should make best use of available synergies there can be considerable wastage of effort and resources if business units are working against each other.

To overcome the fiefdoms is difficult. They often have historical circumstance and folklore to sustain them. Nonetheless the attempt needs to be made to merge the interests of the corporate with the team. Vital to this process is the inclusion of the fiefdoms in the initial research programme as defined in this book. This provides the opportunity to understand different perspectives and to build consensus through the process. The actual brand articulation also needs to be inclusive so that it encompasses the needs of the component parts of the organization. There will certainly be no buy-in to the corporate cause if people can turn their backs on the brand and say 'well it doesn't apply to my team.' The final part of the process is the adaptability of the brand. The workshops and brand champions mechanisms are designed to enable the teams and business units to use the brand to further their own needs – not at the expense of the corporate or other teams, but in harmony with them. For anyone who has lived with long-term fiefdoms, all of this may sound like wishful thinking. It is certainly not an instantaneous process, but from experience I would argue that participation in the above is a genuinely cathartic process, which if sustained can help to bring the sense of the brand more to the fore.

Corporate trauma

Well-articulated and embedded brand ideas can survive corporate traumas. The most often cited example of this is when someone tampered with a pharmaceutical product called Tylenol, which led to fatalities. The brand owner, Johnson & Johnson, was in no way culpable, but it still reacted quickly and resolutely. It withdrew the product immediately, advertised the problem and offered a reward for the capture of the killer. The company was subsequently praised for its handling of the crisis but it claimed that its reactions were made easy by its credo, which defines the way the organization should behave and outlines its responsibilities to society. It is in this sort of instance where a clear brand idea is a powerful touchstone for behaviour. Yet there are instances when the brand has to be modified. The most notable examples of this are when organizations are involved in mergers and acquisitions (M&As). The occasion of an M&A, as any merger psychologist or employee who has been through the process will tell you, is one of tremendous uncertainty. The reputation of acquisitions is not overly positive. In about two-thirds of cases the acquirer's stock price falls immediately after the deal is announced. A presage of worse to come:

> The market's routinely negative response to M&A announcements reflects investors' skepticism about the likelihood that the acquirer will be able both to maintain the original values of the businesses in question and to achieve the synergies required to justify the premium.[7]

Part of the problem is that organizations rarely seem to take the issue of culture into account. Bringing together different cultures and brands is inevitably fraught with problems. If two competitors with distinctive cultures come together, the employees of the respective companies may see the other as enemies or at least polar opposites in terms of belief and attitude. The ill-fated merger between Chrysler and Daimler Benz, where the joint stock valuation of Daimler Chrysler in 2000 was less than Daimler Benz alone prior to the merger (in 1998), is an example. The potential synergies were seen to be enormous, yet so far the two brands have been run separately and the culture clash between the Germans and the Americans has been the most newsworthy feature of the marriage.

To manage the brand identification issue in M&As requires both sensitivity and courage. After the announcement the anxiety of employees can lead to fear about jobs and security, but it also raises questions about how people's lives, post-acquisition, will be in terms of the higher Maslowian needs. Will there still be the opportunity for self actualization? The danger is that employees will use the brand idea as a defence mechanism; that the strength of identification increases and becomes a shield to prevent integration. This is not so much a problem in a portfolio approach, such as operated by marketing services group WPP, but it can be destructive in an integrated organization. To create identification, both sides have to benefit. One company many benefit by acquiring a new skill base, and the other might acquire global reach. If the cultural compatibility is strong it may be possible to fashion a brand idea that is closely related to both organizations' previous existences. However, there may be value in undertaking a brand review programme as described in this book, which enables people to look again at the merged brand and to reach a new consensus on its meaning. If this is to be a genuine fusion, then the groups that come together to stimulate integration need to include members of both organizations and they need to be as objective as possible in formulating both a new way of working and a brand idea that is not the imposition of a set of values by one organization on the other, but a genuine statement of intent. To facilitate this environment is difficult because it is a time of suspicion and what is required is trust. This points to the importance of signalling by management. On these occasions, employees will look at management signals with greater scrutiny; they will be trying to deconstruct memos and announcements to spot the real intent. Management therefore need to be scrupulous in its statements, and above all consistent. Certainly, one of the big issues in the Daimler Chrysler marriage was its original description as a merger of equals and the subsequent statement of Daimler's intention to reduce Chyrsler to a division of Daimler.

The point to recognize in this phase of trauma is that identification with the new merged brand is unlikely to be instantaneous. Like any relationship it will take time to develop. The important thing is to lay good foundations that can be proven by experience.

Whose responsibility?

The complexities of brand management require that the person responsible for articulating and sustaining the brand should have a broad organizational view. If the brand is to be lived by all employees it cannot be the responsibility of someone with a narrow perspective.

In most organizations the title of the person managing this process is chief executive or communications director. However, it could be the human resources or training director or indeed anyone at a senior level. This seniority is important because, perversely, in most organizations genuine participation is only possible if someone with a senior role encourages it. There is also enormous value in obtaining senior management buy-in if commitment and resources are to be maintained over time. Quite often this requires the perseverance of the commissioner of the programme, not only to sustaining the interest of employees but also the enthusiasm of managers.

The title of the individual may not be especially important but his or her knowledge and personality will be. The ideal manager has to be possessed of sufficient credibility and authority to obtain support and sufficient humility to involve and promote others. Some commentators are sceptical of the real value of empowerment. Certainly, empowerment has to have some degree of focus; it does require the duality of freedom and order if it is to succeed. This suggests that the manager needs to be capable of setting a direction and knowing when to take action to ensure effective resolution to issues. Deciding on the brand idea cannot be a perennial talking shop; for example, it requires someone to set limits and to persuade others when decisions have been taken. Simultaneously the programme manager needs to suppress a desire to control. The process should be one of mentoring not imposition.

Summary

Managing the brand is a long-term process, which suggests that the brand idea needs to enter the systems of the organization rather than being the crusade of a lone individual. While the commitment and enthusiasm of certain people will be fundamental to the initial embedding there is no guarantee that those individuals will have the same jobs or responsibilities in the future. Thus the importance of brand workshops and champions in sustaining the brand and the responsibility of individuals to use the brand in their day-to-day work. The relative commitment of individuals will vary depending on their degree of identification with the brand. Overall the stronger the identification the better from the organizational viewpoint, but there are dangers of cultism attached to this. The downside of cults is that they tend to get too inwardly focused and they also lose the ability to question. In managing the brand it is important that questioning and an outward focus are maintained.

Notes

1 Reichheld, F (1993) Loyalty based management, *Harvard Business Review,* (March–April), p 63.
2 Schumacher, E (1974) *Small is Beautiful: A study of economics as if people mattered,* Sphere Books, London.
3 Hamel, Gary (2000) Reinvent your company, *Fortune,* **141** (12) (June 12), pp 170–72.
4 Motorola calculated that for every dollar that it spent on education it received a return of $33 – Gogan, Janis; Zuboff, Shoshana; Schuck, Gloria and Handel, Michael. Motorola: Institutionalising Corporate Initiatives, *Harvard Business Review* (1994).
5 Research by Geert Hofstede into the work-related values and attitudes of 72,000 IBM employees in 40 countries indicates that values are culturally determined. Countries such as the United States, Netherlands and Britain are more individualist and Germany, Spain and Portugal are more collectivist.
6 Eric Hoffer's study of totalitarianism – *The True Believer: Thoughts on the nature of mass movements* (reissued 1989, Harper Perennial) – shows how certainty (one right way of doing things) leads to fanaticism.
7 Rappaport, Alfred and Sirowen, Mark (1999) Stock or cash? The trade-offs for buyers and sellers in mergers and acquisitions. Section entitled: Why the market is skeptical about acquisitions, *Harvard Business Review,* (November–December), p 149.

ten

Conclusion

The aim of this book has been to demonstrate the power of living brands and to suggest ways in which organizations can harness the potential enthusiasm and commitment of their employees to deliver them. In so doing I have made some assumptions. I have assumed that, given the opportunity, most people will want and try to find meaning in their working lives. I have assumed that people will want to work for organizations that have clearly defined and appealing brand ideas. I have assumed that most organizations will want to use the collective intellectual resources at their disposal. And, I have assumed that at least some organizations will be willing to invest time and money in building the skills and knowledge of their people.

None of these seem dangerous assumptions. Yet there are organizations that will eschew these ideas, such as businesses with charismatic leaders or family-owned enterprises that set the organizational goals and the strategy and then pull the organization along with them. Or, there are organizations that have clear and rigid standards that people adhere to and have proven to be successful over time. Some people may find the certainty attached to these role models appealing. There is none of the uncertainty one can associate with empowerment and often these businesses can move at real speed and take advantage of market opportunities. It would be wrong to deny the validity of these more systematic and top-down approaches. They have worked for the best part of the 20th century.

Yet there are implicit constraints. People have changed and have become more demanding of their employment relationships. The pervasiveness of information technology in most organizations has broken down the control of knowledge and made information accessible to everyone. The nature of business has changed, so that access to intellect and creativity has become the key route to competitive advantage. Organizations are becoming larger and more global in their orientation. Collectively these factors make top down management harder to sustain, particularly in an organization of any size. If one accepts the idea of a more participative approach to organizational management – and hopefully the arguments have been persuasive – then the fundamental task must be to engage people with what they spend their days doing. This suggests that brand ideas have to be capable of being:

- imaginative;
- authentic;
- courageous;
- empowering.

Being imaginative

To create meaning in our working lives we need to believe in the value of what we do. For most people brand statements that stress ideas connected with cost or profitability will not be ultimately engaging. This does not deny the power of monetary reward but it does indicate that brand ideas have to make an emotional appeal to our larger goals as human beings. For this reason, the most significant brands have strongly emotive elements. They tap into our need to feel good about what we do, to build our self-esteem and our ideas of self-actualization. These 'big ideas' provide an arena within which employees can innovate. Rather than unfocused creativity, as the Shakespearean analogy of *Romeo and Juliet* demonstrated, well-articulated ideas provide the boundaries of imagination. From a management perspective, this enables empowerment programmes to be instituted – such as the Unipart example below – in the confidence that they will be in line with the brand idea. Referring to learning within the organization, Unipart says that the techniques 'must be addressed within the Context of the Group's mission and values to ensure acceptance, understanding and commitment from employees.' In other words, such is the relevance of the brand idea in this organization that employees will not accept or commit to new things unless they match their view of the brand.

Think back to the opening chapter of this book and the story of Patagonia. This brand touches the lives of the people that work for the organization with a set of values that stir their imaginations; that suggest they can create a better world. In so doing it builds a huge sense of commitment and enthusiasm. Chip Bell is a powerful metaphor for this because, as he suggests, there is a seamless link between his home and working life. He does not have to pretend to be one thing on the way to work and another when he gets there. The imaginative quality of the Patagonia brand in turn touches its customers and partners and is cemented through the storytelling that pervades the brand. It is difficult to imagine someone developing a new product or service in Patagonia that is conventional, non-functional and environmentally damaging. People would not allow it to happen.

Of course, the power of such a brand can also be dangerous. It can mean people ignore opportunities. It can also mean we're more disappointed when the brand fails to perform. Brand ideas, because they are developed and delivered by people, will disappoint us. Those negative 'moments of truth' will occasionally surface, but the more consistent the brand is, the fewer the disappointments and the more forgiving we can be.

Being authentic

Authenticity is a widely used word in business. However, authenticity relates to both words and actions. Authenticity of language is important because it signals to us as both employees and customers that we can trust what an organization says. In some ways this is the antithesis of traditional marketing, which has always tended to stress the positives, ignore the negatives and indulge in hyperbole. Occasionally brands have made a virtue of communicating that 'they tell it like it is' but the inference of this is that if you need to say it there is a lack of overall authenticity in the market. Self-consciously using down-to-earth language in a marketing context means that someone has made an explicit decision to take advantage of a market opportunity.

The need for real authenticity is driven by two factors. First, the Web has opened up a potential for dialogue, which means that consumers can share their experiences about brands and employees can more easily share their ideas with each other. There is no mediation in this conversation. People say what they really think. The introduction of inauthentic language, especially in the digital arena, suddenly looks very out of place. Second, companies are more exposed than ever before. Consumers want to see behind companies and to understand what they are really like. There is no hiding place. This connects to the other facet of authenticity – actions. Whatever the language used, employees and other audiences are too knowing to be fooled for long. A company initiative that claims a new way of thinking will soon founder if it is not supported by actions. Authenticity means saying what you do and doing what you say in a language and a manner that is credible.

Being courageous

Brands have increasing difficulty in differentiating themselves. The only way they can create a realizable competitive advantage is by having a distinctive point of view. However, stepping outside the norms is highly risky. There is safety in being in the pack. Courage means confronting the anxiety that goes with difficult choices and then committing to the ideas that ensue. Look at the Interbrand rankings of top brands and you will see organizations that have been consistently courageous. There have been some failures – courage has risk attached to it – but there is also a real sense of euphoria for businesses that have shown others a new way of thinking, from Nokia's adoption of design as a point of difference to IBM's reinvention of itself to Dell's systems for product customization.

To build a courageous brand, the brand idea itself has to contain a tension. If the values are simply reinforcing what the organization does well, there is little incentive for experimentation. However, if the values are stretching and pulling the organization, a sense of dynamism emerges. This is part of the value of Koestenbaum's model in that it contains seemingly opposed, centrifugal forces. It is the ability to countenance and live with the anxiety that makes for a strong brand.

Empowering

This is a key concept in the idea of brand articulation and implementation. As a principle, empowerment is important because it uses the full intellectual power of the organization to solve problems. An example of this is Unipart, where any employee can solve a challenge that faces him or her in the workplace by setting up a quality circle. Individuals can choose the people they feel appropriate to the success of the circle and can set their own agenda. Once the project is complete the findings are shared with others. At any one time, approximately a third of the company's workforce is involved in quality circles. Of course, the company could have initiated such programmes itself, but management recognizes that the employees closest to the day-to-day issues are best placed to resolve them.

When it comes to articulating the brand, I can only argue from personal experience and observation. Participative processes that fully engage people do not always produce the best phrased and presented brand definitions, but they do generate robust definitions that are true to the employees of an organization. They can then build a commitment that seems to be rare in processes that are top down or too consultancy heavy. The same argument also goes for implementation.

Articulating a brand is only the beginning. Every brand worth its salt has a brand idea. Only a few seem capable of actually delivering the ideas. That requires commitment from management, the ongoing involvement of employees and continuous analysis, feedback and improvement. The real challenge here is to change a manager's mindset away from an approach that focuses on selling an idea to others in the organization to a more organic method, which following the planting of a seed of an idea, grows through the involvement and enthusiasm of others.

Index